Bruce Levin

About the Author

ROSS W. GREENE, PH.D., is Associate Professor of Psychology in the Department of Psychiatry at Harvard Medical School and Founding Director of the Collaborative Problem Solving Institute in the Department of Psychiatry at Massachusetts General Hospital. Dr. Greene's research focuses on the classification and treatment of explosive children and adolescents and their families; the classification, longitudinal study, and treatment of severe social impairment in children with ADHD; and the influence of teacher characteristics on school outcome for elementary school students with disruptive behavior disorders. He has authored numerous articles, chapters, and scientific papers on school- and home-based interventions for children with disruptive behavior disorders; behavioral assessment and social functioning in children; eliminating restraint and seclusion procedures in therapeutic day schools, inpatient units, and residential and juvenile detention facilities; and student-teacher compatibility. Dr. Greene's research has been funded by the Stanley Medical Research Institute, the National Institute on Drug Abuse, and the U.S. Department of Education.

Dr. Greene received his doctorate in clinical psychology from Virginia Tech in 1989 after completing his predoctoral internship at Children's National Medical Center in Washington, D.C. Prior to his current positions, he served as Visiting Assistant Professor on the clinical psychology faculty at Virginia Tech and as Assistant Professor in Psychiatry and in Pediatrics at University of Massachusetts Medical Center. He lives outside Boston with his wife, daughter, and son.

The Explosive Child

The Explosive Child

A New Approach for Understanding and Parenting Easily Frustrated, Chronically Inflexible Children

Ross W. Greene, Ph.D.

Harper
An Imprint of HarperCollins*Publishers*

HarperCollins books may be purchased for educational, business, or sales promotional use. For information please write: Special Markets Department, HarperCollins Publishers, 10 East 53rd Street, New York, NY 10022.

FIRST HARPER PAPERBACK PUBLISHED 2005.

Designed by Phil Mazzone

Library of Congress Cataloging-in-Publication Data is available upon request.

ISBN-10: 0-06-077939-X
ISBN-13: 978-0-06-077939-9

07 08 09 ❖/RRD 10 9

In memory of Irving A. Greene

Anyone can become angry, that is easy . . .
but to be angry with the right person, to the right degree, at the right time, for the right purpose, and in the right way . . . this is not easy.

—Aristotle

If I am not for myself, who is for me?
If I am only for myself, what am I?
If not now, when?

—Hillel

Illusions are the truths we live by until we know better.

—Nancy Gibbs

Contents

Acknowledgments

I would like to acknowledge the contributions of my valued colleague and friend, Dr. Stuart Ablon, whose insights and energy have been instrumental in the evolution of the Collaborative Problem Solving approach. I am also indebted, as always, to my agent and friend, Wendy Lipkind.

My thinking about how to help explosive children and their adult caretakers has been influenced by many parents, teachers, and supervisors. It was my incredible good fortune to have been mentored by Dr. Thomas Ollendick while I was a graduate student in the clinical psychology program at Virginia Tech. Two psychologists who supervised me during my training years were particularly influential: Drs. George Clum at Virginia Tech and Mary Ann McCabe at Children's National Medical Center in Washington, D.C. And I probably wouldn't have gone into psychology in the first place if I hadn't stumbled across the path of Dr. Elizabeth Altmaier when I was an undergraduate at the University of Florida.

However, those who were most central to the evolution of many of the ideas in this book, and to whom I owe the greatest debt of gratitude, were the many children with whom I've worked and the parents who entrusted me with their care.

I also want to acknowledge the countless people throughout the world who have embraced the Collaborative Problem Solving approach and, against the odds but with vision and energy and relentless determination, have advocated for implementation of the approach in their schools, clinics, inpatient units, and residential and juvenile detention facilities. There are truly amazing people in this world who care deeply about improving the lives of children, and it has been my privilege to have crossed paths with many of you.

This book is about children and families, and I'd be remiss if I didn't acknowledge my own: my wife, Melissa; my kids, Talia and Jacob, who keep me laughing and learning and make sure I practice what I preach; and Sandy, the Big Black Dog.

While there are many explosive girls, for ease of exposition most of this book is written in the masculine gender. The names and identifying information of all the children in this book are completely fictitious. Any resemblance to actual children of the same names is, as the saying goes, purely coincidental.

Preface

Welcome to the third edition of *The Explosive Child.* Much has happened since the first edition was published in 1998. To begin with, the approach described in these pages now has a name: Collaborative Problem Solving (CPS). And to make it easier for people to understand and implement, there have also been a variety of updates to the model, and these changes are presented in this edition. And there's now a nonprofit organization—the Collaborative Problem Solving Institute—that has been established to help us reach out to more parents, teachers, and others who work with and care about explosive kids. And the Boston Red Sox won the World Series.

This revised edition is still about the same kids: the ones who often exhibit extreme behaviors—intense temper outbursts, noncompliance, verbal and physical aggression—that make life extraordinarily challenging and frustrating for them, their parents, siblings, teachers, and others who interact with them. They have, of course, been described in many ways: difficult, challenging, willful, manipulative, attention-seeking, contrary, intransigent, unmotivated. They may carry any or many of various psychiatric diagnoses, such as oppositional-defiant disorder (ODD), attention-deficit/hyperactivity disorder (ADHD), intermittent explosive disorder, Tourette's disorder, depression, bipolar disorder, nonverbal learning disability, Asperger's disorder, and obsessive-compulsive disorder (OCD). But their behavior has typically been very poorly understood.

For a long time the prevailing view of such behavior has been that it is the by-product of inept parenting practices. But research of the past two decades suggests that the difficulties of explosive children are a lot more complex than previously thought and may emanate from a variety of different factors. We've learned a lot about children's brains in the last twenty years; it's time for what we do to help them to be a reflection of what we now know about them. By the way, while the title of this book suggests that the content is relevant only to children who explode, the CPS model is applicable equally to children who withdraw, cry, or "implode."

In writing this and the first two editions of *The Explosive Child*, my goal has been to provide an enlightened understanding of the children and, flowing from this understanding, to describe a practical, comprehensive approach aimed at decreasing adversarial interactions between explosive children and their adult caretakers at home and in school.

The kids haven't changed all that much since I worked with my first explosive child a long time ago, but my approach to helping them and their parents and teachers is a lot different. And it works a lot better.

As always, the only prerequisite is an open mind.

The Explosive Child

1

The Waffle Episode

Jennifer, age eleven, wakes up, makes her bed, looks around her room to make sure everything is in its place, and heads into the kitchen to make herself breakfast. She peers into the freezer, removes the container of frozen waffles, and counts six waffles. Thinking to herself, "I'll have three waffles this morning and three tomorrow morning," Jennifer toasts her three waffles and sits down to eat.

Moments later her mother and five-year-old brother, Adam, enter the kitchen, and the mother asks Adam what he'd like to eat for breakfast. Adam responds, "Waffles," and the mother reaches into the freezer for the waffles. Jennifer, who has been listening intently, explodes.

"He can't have the frozen waffles!" Jennifer screams, her face suddenly reddening.

"Why not?" asks the mother, her voice and pulse rising, at a loss for an explanation of Jennifer's behavior.

"I was going to have those waffles tomorrow morning!" Jennifer screams, jumping out of her chair.

"I'm not telling your brother he can't have waffles!" the mother yells back.

"He can't have them!" screams Jennifer, now face-to-face with her mother.

The mother, wary of the physical and verbal aggression of which her daughter is capable during these moments, desperately asks Adam if there might be something else he would consider eating.

"I want waffles," Adam whimpers, cowering behind his mother.

Jennifer, her frustration and agitation at a peak, pushes her mother out of the way, seizes the container of frozen waffles, then slams the freezer door shut, pushes over a kitchen chair, grabs her plate of toasted waffles, and stalks to her room. Her brother and mother begin to cry.

Jennifer's family members have endured thousands of such explosions. In many instances, the explosions are more prolonged and intense, involving more physical or verbal aggression than the one described above (when Jennifer was eight, she kicked out the front windshield of the family car). Mental health professionals have bestowed myriad diagnoses upon Jennifer: oppositional-defiant disorder, bipolar disorder, intermittent explosive disorder. For the parents, however, a simple label doesn't begin to explain the upheaval, turmoil, and trauma that Jennifer's outbursts cause.

Her siblings and mother are scared of her. Her extreme volatility and inflexibility require constant vigilance and enormous energy from her mother and father, thereby detracting from the attention the parents wish they could devote to Jennifer's brother and sister. Her parents frequently argue over the best way to handle her behavior, but they agree about the severe strains Jennifer places on their marriage. Although she is above average in intelligence, Jennifer has no close friends; children who initially befriend her eventually find her rigid personality difficult to tolerate.

Over the years Jennifer's parents have sought help from countless mental health professionals, most of whom advised them to set firmer limits and be more consistent in managing Jennifer's behavior, and instructed them on how to implement formal reward and punishment strategies, usually in the form of sticker charts and time-outs. When such strategies failed to work, Jennifer was medicated with innumerable combinations of drugs, without dramatic effect. After eight years of disparate advice, firmer limits, medicine, and motivational programs, Jennifer has changed little since her parents first noticed there was something "different" about her when she was a toddler.

"Most people can't imagine how humiliating it is to be scared of your own daughter," Jennifer's mother once said. "People who don't have a child like Jennifer don't have a clue about what it's like to live like this. Believe me, this is not what I envisioned when I dreamed of having children. This is a nightmare.

"You can't imagine the embarrassment of having Jennifer 'lose it' around people who don't know her," her mother continued. "I feel like telling them, 'I have two kids at home who don't act like this—I really am a good parent!'

"I know people are thinking, 'What wimpy parents she must have . . . what that kid really needs is a good thrashing.' Believe me, we've tried everything with her. But nobody's been able to tell us how to help her . . . no one's really been able to tell us what's the matter with her!

"I hate what I've become. I used to think of myself as a kind, patient, sympathetic person. But Jennifer has caused me to act in ways in which I never thought myself capable. I'm emotionally spent. I can't keep living like this.

"I know a lot of other parents who have pretty difficult children . . . you know, kids who are hyperactive or having trouble paying attention. I would give my left arm for a kid who was just hyperactive or having trouble paying attention! Jennifer is in a completely different league! It makes me feel very alone."

The truth is that Jennifer's mother is not alone; there are a lot of Jennifers out there. Their parents often discover that strategies that are usually effective for shaping the behavior of other children—such as explaining, reasoning, reassuring, nurturing, redirecting, insisting, ignoring, rewarding, and punishing—don't achieve the same success with their Jennifers. Even commonly prescribed medications often do not lead to satisfactory improvement. If you started reading this book because you have a Jennifer of your own, you're probably familiar with how frustrated, confused, angry, bitter, guilty, overwhelmed, worn-out, and hopeless Jennifer's parents feel.

Besides the diagnoses mentioned above, children like Jennifer may be diagnosed with any of a variety of other psychiatric conditions and learning inefficiencies, including attention-deficit/hyperactivity disorder (ADHD), depression, Tourette's disorder, anxiety disorders (including obsessive-compulsive disorder), language-processing impairments, sensory integration dysfunction, nonverbal learning disability (NLD), reactive attachment disorder, and Asperger's disorder. Such children may also be described as having difficult temperaments. Whatever the label, children like Jennifer are distinguished by a few characteristics—namely, striking inflexibility and poor frustration tolerance—that make life significantly more difficult and challenging for them and for the people who interact with them. These children have enormous difficulty thinking things through when they become frustrated and often respond to even simple changes and requests with extreme rigidity and often verbal or physical aggression. For ease of exposition, throughout this book I'll refer to these children as "explosive," but the approach described in this book is equally applicable to "implosive" kids—those whose inflexibility and poor tolerance for frustration cause them to shut down and withdraw.

How are explosive children different from other kids? Let's take a look at how different children may respond to a fairly common family scenario. Imagine that Child 1—Hubert—is watching television and his mother asks him to set the table for dinner. Hubert has a pretty easy time shifting from his agenda—watching television—to his mother's agenda—setting the table for dinner. Thus, in response to, "Hubert, I'd like you to turn off the television and come set the table for dinner," he would likely reply, "OK, Mom, I'm coming," and would set about the task of fulfilling his mother's request.

Child 2—Jermaine—is a little tougher. He has a harder time shifting from his agenda to his mother's agenda but is able to manage his frustration and shift gears (sometimes with the assistance of a threat hanging over his head). Thus, in response to "Jermaine, I'd like you to turn off the television and come set the table for dinner," Jermaine might initially shout, "No way, I don't want to right now!" or complain, "You always ask me to do things right when I'm in the middle of something I like!" However, with some extra help (Mother: "Jermaine, if you don't turn off the television and come set the dinner table right now, you're going to have to take a time-out"), these "somewhat tougher" children do shift gears.

And then there is Jennifer, Child 3, the explosive child, for whom demands for shifting gears—from her agenda to her mother's agenda—often induce a fairly rapid, intense, debilitating level of frustration. In response to "Jennifer, I'd like you to turn off the television and come set the table for dinner," these children get stuck and often eventually explode (even with a threat hanging over their heads), at which point all bets are off on what they may say or do.

Explosive children come in all shapes and sizes. Some blow up dozens of times every day; others only a few times a week. Many "lose it" only at home, others only at school, some both at home and at school. Some scream when they become frustrated but do not swear or become physically or verbally aggressive. One such child, Richard, a spunky, charismatic fourteen-year-old who was diagnosed with ADHD, began to cry in our first session when I asked if he thought it might be a good idea for us to help him start managing his frustration so he could begin getting along better with his family members. Others scream and swear but do not lash out physically, including Jack, an engaging, smart, moody ten-year-old, diagnosed with ADHD and Tourette's disorder, who had a very reliable pattern of becoming inflexible and irrational over the most trivial matters and whose swearing and screaming in the midst of frustration tended to elicit similar behaviors from his parents. Still others combine the whole package, such as Marvin, a bright, active, impulsive, edgy, easily agitated eight-year-old diagnosed with Tourette's disorder, depression, and ADHD, who reacted to unexpected changes with unimaginable intensity (and occasional physical violence). On one occasion, Marvin's father innocently turned off an unnecessary light in the room in which Marvin was playing a video game, prompting a massive one-hour blowup.

What should become quite clear as you read this book is that these children have wonderful qualities and tremendous potential. In most ways, their general cognitive skills have developed at a normal pace. Yet their inflexibility and poor tolerance for frustration often obscure their more positive traits and cause them and those around them enormous pain. There is no other group of children who are so misunderstood. Their parents are typically caring, well-intentioned people, who often feel guilty that they haven't been able to help their children.

"You know," Jennifer's mother would say, "each time I start to get my hopes up . . . each time I have a pleasant interaction with Jennifer . . . I let myself become a little optimistic and start to like her again . . . and then it all comes crashing down with her next explosion. I'm ashamed to say it, but a lot of the time I really don't like her and I definitely don't like what she's doing to our family. We are in a perpetual state of crisis."

Clearly, there's something different about the Jennifers of the world. This is a critical realization for their parents and other caretakers to come to. But there is hope, as long as their parents, teachers, relatives, and therapists are able to come to grips with a second realization: Explosive children often require a different approach to discipline and limit setting than do other children.

Dealing more effectively with explosive children requires, first and foremost, an understanding of why these children behave as they do. Once this understanding is achieved, strategies for helping things improve often become self-evident. In some instances, achieving a more accurate understanding of a child's difficulties can, by itself, lead to improvements in adult-child interactions, even before any formal strategies are tried. The first chapters of this book are devoted to helping you think about why these children adapt so poorly to changes and requests, are so easily frustrated, and explode so quickly and so often. Along the way, you'll read about why popular strategies for dealing with difficult children are often less effective than expected. In later chapters, you'll read about alternative strategies that have been helpful to many of the children, families, and teachers with whom I've worked over the years.

If you are the parent of an explosive child, this book may restore some sanity and optimism to your family and help you feel that you can actually handle your child's difficulties confidently and competently. If you are a relative, friend, teacher, or therapist, this book should, at the least, help you understand. There is no panacea. But there is cause for optimism and hope.

2

Children Do Well If They Can

One of the most amazing and gratifying things about being a parent is watching your child develop new skills and master increasingly complex tasks with each passing month and year. Crawling progresses to walking and then advances to running; babbling slowly develops into full-blown talking; smiling progresses to more sophisticated forms of socialization; learning the letters of the alphabet sets the stage for reading whole words and then sentences, paragraphs, and books.

It is also amazing how unevenly different children's

skills develop. Some children learn to read more readily than they learn to do math. Some children turn out to be excellent athletes, whereas others may be less athletically skilled. In some cases, skills may lag because of a child's lack of exposure to the material (for example, maybe Steve can't hit a baseball very well because no one ever showed him how to do it). More commonly, children have difficulty learning a particular skill even though they have the desire to master the skill and have been provided with the instruction typically needed to master it. It's not that they don't want to learn; it's simply that they are not learning as readily as expected. When children's skills in a particular area lag well behind their expected development, we often give them special help, as when Steve's baseball coach provided batting instruction or Ken's school gave him remedial assistance in reading.

Just as some children lag in acquiring reading or athletic skills, others—the children this book is about—do not progress to the degree we would have hoped in the domains of *flexibility* and *frustration tolerance*. Mastery of these skills is crucial to a child's overall development because interacting adaptively with the world requires the continual ability to solve problems, work out disagreements, and control the emotions one experiences when frustrated. Indeed, it's difficult to imagine many situations in a child's day that don't require flexibility, adaptability, and frustration tolerance. When two children disagree about which game to play, we hope both children possess the skills to resolve the dispute in a mutually satisfactory manner. When bad weather forces parents to cancel their child's much-anticipated trip to the amusement park, we hope the child has the ability to express his disappointment appropriately, shift gears, and settle on an alternative plan. When a child is engrossed in a video game and it's time to come to dinner, we hope the child is able to interrupt his game, manage his understandable feelings of frustration, and think clearly enough to recognize that he can return to the game later. And when a child decides she'll have three frozen waffles for breakfast today and three tomorrow and her younger brother decides he wants three frozen waffles today, too, we hope the child can move beyond black-and-white thinking ("I am definitely going to have those three waffles for breakfast tomorrow so there's no way my brother can have them") and recognize the gray in the situation ("I guess I don't have to eat those exact waffles . . . I can ask my mom to buy more . . . anyway, I might not even feel like eating waffles tomorrow").

Some children are inflexible and easily frustrated from the moment they pop into the world. For example, infants with difficult temperaments may be colicky, have irregular sleep patterns, have difficulties with feeding, may be difficult to comfort or soothe, may overreact to noises, lights, and discomfort (hunger, cold, a wet diaper, etc.), and respond poorly to changes. Other children may not begin to have difficulty with flexibility and frustration tolerance until later, when demands increase for skills such as language, organization, impulse control, regulation of emotions, and social skills.

Here's the important point: The children about whom this book is written do not *choose* to be explosive—any more than a child would choose to have a reading disability—but they are delayed in the process of developing the skills essential for flexibility and frustration tolerance. It follows that conventional explanations as to why children explode or refuse to do as they are told—"He's doing it for attention"; "He just wants his own way"; "He's manipulating us"; "He could do better if he really wanted to"; "He does just fine when he chooses to"—miss the mark. There's a big difference between viewing explosive behavior as the result of the failure to progress developmentally and viewing it as learned, planned, intentional, goal-oriented, and purposeful. That's because your interpretation of a child's explosive behavior will be closely linked to how you try to change this behavior. In other words, *your explanation guides your intervention*.

This theme is worth thinking about for a moment. If you interpret a child's behavior as planned, intentional, goal-oriented, and purposeful, then labels such as "stubborn," "willful," "intransigent," "manipulative," "bratty," "attention-seeking," "controlling," "resistant," "unmotivated," "out of control," and "defiant" will sound perfectly reasonable to you, and popular strategies aimed at motivating compliant behavior and "teaching the child who's boss" will make perfect sense. If this has been your explanation of your child's explosive behavior, you're not alone. You're also not alone if this explanation and the interventions that flow from it haven't led you to a productive outcome.

Throughout this book, I encourage you to put conventional "wisdom" on the shelf and give some consideration to the alternative explanation: that your child is already very motivated to do well and that his explosive behavior reflects a developmental delay—a learning disability of sorts—in the skills of flexibility and frustration tolerance. From this perspective, putting a lot of energy into motivating your child and teaching him who's boss may actually be counterproductive, since he's already motivated and already knows who's boss.

So is there a better way to understand these children? Are there more accurate ways of describing their difficulties? And are there alternative strategies that may better match the needs of explosive children and their families?

Yes, yes, and yes.

Let's start with the understanding part. The single most important theme of this book is as follows:

Children do well if they can.

In other words, if your child could do well, he would do well. If he could handle disagreements and adults setting limits and the demands being placed on him without exploding, he'd do it. And now you know why he can't do it: He has a learning disability in the domains of flexibility and frustration tolerance. How did he get that way? It turns out that there are some specific skills he's probably lacking. More details on these skills in the next chapter. What can we do to help him? Ah, that's what the rest of the book is about.

The problem is that a very different philosophy—*Children do well if they want to*—often guides adults' thinking in their interactions with explosive children. Adherents to this idea believe children are already capable of behaving more appropriately but simply don't want to. And why don't they want to? The knee-jerk explanation—even among many well-intentioned mental health professionals—is that *their parents are poor disciplinarians*. Of course this explanation doesn't help us understand why many of the siblings of explosive children are actually very well behaved. But, as you'd expect, this philosophy and explanation lead to interventions aimed at making children want to do well and helping parents become more effective disciplinarians, typically through implementation of popular reward and punishment programs. More on why these programs often don't get the job done in chapter 5.

Let's move on to the describing part. Rule number one: Don't place a lot of faith in psychiatric diagnoses to help you understand your explosive child. Diagnoses don't help you identify the compromised thinking skills underlying your child's explosive outbursts. Saying that a child "has ADHD" or "has bipolar disorder" or "has obsessive-compulsive disorder" gives us no information whatever about the thinking skills a child is lacking that we adults need to help him develop.

Better than any diagnosis, here's a description that helps people understand what's happening when a child (or an adult, for that matter) explodes:

An explosive outburst—like other forms of maladaptive behavior—occurs when the cognitive demands being placed upon a person outstrip that person's capacity to respond adaptively.

You won't find this description in any diagnostic manual (I wouldn't worry about that too much). It's actually a good description of the vast majority of maladaptive behaviors human beings exhibit. It's why people have panic attacks. It's why a child might refuse to sleep in his own bedroom at night. It's why a child might crawl under a desk and curl up in a fetal position. But in the case of the kids this book is about—the explosive ones—it's why they explode. Now we just have to figure out which factors are hindering *your* child's capacity to respond adaptively to the demands for flexibility and frustration tolerance being placed upon him.

Nothing is more frustrating for a parent than having a child with a chronic problem that is not yet fully understood. If your child has chronic stomachaches, chronic headaches, a bad case of eczema, difficulty breathing, you want to know why! And if your child has chronic difficulties tolerating frustration and handling demands for flexibility, you want to know why! In their own incredible frustration and confusion over their child's explosions, parents frequently demand that the child provide a logical explanation for his actions. In general, your child would be the wrong person to ask. So the dialogue often goes something like this:

Parent: "We've talked about this a million times . . . WHY DON'T YOU DO WHAT YOU'RE TOLD? WHAT ARE YOU SO ANGRY ABOUT?"
Explosive child: "I don't know."

The child's maddening response usually has the effect of further heightening his parents' frustration. It's worth noting, of course, that the child is probably telling the truth.

In a perfect world the child would respond with something like, "See, Mom and Dad, I have this little problem. You guys—and lots of other people—are constantly telling me what to do or demanding that I shift from how I was thinking to how you're thinking, and I'm not very good at it. In fact, when you ask me to do these things, I start to get frustrated. And when I start getting frustrated, I have trouble thinking clearly and then I get even more frustrated. Then you guys get mad. Then I start doing things I wish I didn't do and saying things I wish I didn't say. Then you guys get even madder and punish me, and it gets really messy. After the dust settles—you know, when I start thinking clearly again—I end up being really sorry for the things I did and said. I know this isn't fun for you, but rest assured, I'm not having any fun either."

Alas, we live in an imperfect world. Explosive children are rarely able to describe their difficulties with this kind of clarity. However, some kids and adults are pretty articulate about what happens in the midst of explosions. One child referred to how his brain got stuck in the midst of frustration as "brain lock." He explained that he locked on to an idea and then had tremendous difficulty unlocking, regardless of how reasonable or rational the attempts of others to unlock him. Another computer-savvy child said he wished his brain had a Pentium processor so he could think faster and more efficiently when he became frustrated. Dr. Daniel Goleman, author of *Emotional Intelligence*, referred to explosions as a "neural hijacking." It's pretty clear that when a child is in the midst of an explosion, there's "nobody home." Our goals, of course, are to make sure that your child's brain doesn't get locked up or his neurons hijacked; to help him think more clearly and efficiently in the midst of frustration; and to make sure there's somebody at home.

You've just been given a lot of new ideas to digest. Here's a quick summary of the main points:

- Flexibility and frustration tolerance are critical developmental skills that some children fail to develop at an age-appropriate pace. Inadequate development of these skills can contribute to a variety of behaviors—sudden outbursts, explosions, and physical and verbal aggression, often in response to what might seem the most benign or trivial of circumstances—that have a traumatic, adverse impact on these children's interactions and relationships with parents, teachers, siblings, and peers.

- How you explain your child's explosive behavior and the language you use to describe it will directly influence the strategies you use to help your child change this behavior.

- Putting conventional explanations on the shelf will also mean putting conventional parenting practices on the shelf. You need a new plan. But first you've got some figuring out to do.

3

Pathways and Triggers

A few important things need to happen if we are to reduce or eliminate your child's explosions. If it's true that *children do well if they can,* then first and foremost we must achieve an understanding of the precise factors that are making it hard for your child to do well. In other words, we need to identify the factors that are compromising his skills in the domains of flexibility and frustration tolerance. In this chapter we'll take a closer look at the specific "pathways" that may set the stage for explosions. Why are they called pathways? Because each category includes specific thinking skills, the absence of which can set the stage for a child to head down the *path* to explosive behavior.

Fortunately, the list of possibilities isn't terribly lengthy: *executive skills, language processing skills, emotion regulation skills, cognitive flexibility skills,* and *social skills*. But there are a few things you should notice about this list before we jump in. First, notice that all the categories end with the same word: *skills.* Pathways can best be thought of as *skills that need to be trained*. Second, reward and punishment programs don't train the child in any of these skills. That's right: You don't train executive skills, language skills, emotion regulation skills, cognitive flexibility skills, or social skills with sticker charts or time-outs. Third, there are no diagnoses on the list. You already know why: Diagnoses aren't very useful at helping you identify the thinking skills your child is lacking. Finally, "inept parenting" and "poor discipline" are not on the list. Inept parenting and poor discipline aren't the reasons your child is lacking skills in the domains of flexibility and frustration tolerance.

Identifying your child's pathways accomplishes several crucial missions. First, if you're able to pinpoint lacking thinking skills that are contributing to your child's difficulties, it's unlikely that you (or anyone else, if you're persuasive) will continue explaining his behavior as attention-seeking, manipulative, or unmotivated. Second, identifying your child's pathways will help make explosions much more predictable. Finally, if you know

what thinking skills your child is lacking, y
actly the thinking skills that need to be taug

EXECUTIVE SKILLS

Executive skills—including *shifting cognitive set* (the ability to shift efficiently from one mind-set to another), *organization and planning* (organizing a coherent plan of action to deal with a problem or frustration), and *separation of affect* (the ability to separate your emotional response to a problem from the thinking you need to perform to solve the problem)—are crucial to one's ability to deal effectively with frustration, think flexibly, and solve problems. While these skills are thought to be governed by the frontal, prefrontal, and frontally interconnected subcortical regions of the brain, what's really useful about them is that they help us understand what's going on (or, perhaps more accurately, what's *not* going on) inside the brains of many explosive children. By the way, most kids diagnosed with ADHD have difficulties with executive skills. Let's take a quick look at each skill.

Moving from one environment (such as recess) to a completely different environment (such as a reading class) requires a shift from one mind-set ("in recess it's OK to run around and make noise and socialize") to another ("in reading, we sit at our desks and read quietly and independently"). If a child has difficulty shifting cognitive set, there's a good chance he'll be thinking and acting as if he's still in recess long after reading class has started. In other words, difficulty shifting cognitive set explains why many children have such trouble making transitions from the rules and expectations of one activity to the rules and expectations of another. And difficulty shifting cognitive set may also explain why a child may become stuck when, for example, his parents ask him to stop watching television and come in for dinner. If a child is an inefficient "shifter" and if other factors—like the parents *insisting* that he shift gears quickly—compound his mounting frustration or compromise his capacity for clear thinking, even seemingly simple requests for shifting may set the stage for serious explosions. Such children are not intentionally trying to be noncompliant; rather, they have trouble flexibly and efficiently shifting from one mind-set to another.

Parent: My child does just fine unless something doesn't go the way he thought it would.

Therapist: Precisely.

Parent: Doesn't that mean he just wants his way?

Therapist: We all just want our way. Your child lacks some of the skills he needs to shift from the mind-set he was in to the mind-set you want him to be in.

Parent: So what should I do?

Therapist: Teach those skills.

How do we know a child is having difficulty shifting cognitive set? He tells us! Let's listen in:

Parent: I'm running a little behind today. Finish your breakfast, put your dishes in the sink, and get ready for school.

Child: I'm not through eating yet.

Parent: Why don't you grab an apple or something. Come on, hurry! I have to drop some things at the post office on the way there.

Child: I can't do that!

Parent: You can't do what? Why do you always do this when I'm in a hurry? Just this once, could you please do what I say without arguing?

Child: I don't know what to do!

Parent: I just told you what to do! Don't push me today!

Child: *(Kaboom)*

Can explosive children be helped to shift cognitive set more efficiently? Absolutely. Just not with threats and consequences.

Organization and planning are also critical to the process of thinking through one's options for dealing with problems or frustrations. Children with ADHD, for example, are notorious for being disorganized (trouble bringing the appropriate homework materials home from school, being absentminded, and slow in getting ready for school in the morning) and impulsive (calling out answers in class, difficulty awaiting their turns, and interrupting and intruding on others). However, disorganization and poor planning also explain the difficulty many children have in responding effectively to life's problems and frustrations. What's the main thing your brain must do when faced with a frustration? Solve the problem that frustrated you in the first place. It turns out that problem solving requires a great deal of organization and planning. First, you need to identify the problem you're trying to solve (it's very hard to solve a problem if you don't know what the problem is), then consider a range of possible solutions to the problem, and then anticipate the likely outcomes of those solutions so as to choose a course of action.

Many children are so disorganized in their thinking that they're unable to identify the problem that's frustrating them. Many are so disorganized that they can't think of any more than one solution to a problem. Many are so impulsive that, even if they could think of more than one solution, they've already done the first thing that popped into their heads. The bad news? Your first solution is often your worst. Good solutions require organization and impulse control. So there are a lot of kids out there who are notorious for putting their "worst foot forward." Many of these disorganized, impulsive kids evidence a pattern called reflexive negativity. This refers to the tendency for the child to instantaneously say "No!" every time there's a change in plan or he's presented with a new idea or request.

Can explosive children be helped to approach problems in a more organized, less impulsive manner so they explode less often? Sure thing. But not with sticker charts or time-outs.

Thinking clearly and solving problems is a lot easier if a person has the capacity to separate or detach himself from the emotions caused by frustration, an executive skill sometimes referred to as separation of affect. While emotions can be useful for mobilizing or energizing people to solve a problem, thinking is how problems get solved. The skill of separation of affect permits people to put their emotions "on the shelf" in order to think through solutions to problems more objectively, rationally, and logically. Kids who are pretty good at separating thought from emotion tend to respond to problems or frustrations with more thought than emotion, and that's good. But children whose skills in this domain are lacking tend to respond to problems or frustrations with less thought and more emotion, and that's not so good. They may actually feel themselves "heating up" but often aren't able to stem the emotional tide until later, when the emotions have subsided and rational thought has kicked back in. They may even have the knowledge to deal successfully with problems (under calmer circumstances, they can actually demonstrate such knowledge), but when they're frustrated, their powerful emotions prevent them from accessing and using the information. Such children are not intentionally trying to be noncompliant; rather, they become overwhelmed by the emotions associated with frustration and have difficulty applying rational thought until they calm down. You know what this is like:

Parent: It's time to stop playing Nintendo and get ready for bed.

Child (responding with more emotion than thought): Damn! I'm right in the middle of an important game!

Parent (perhaps also responding with more emotion than thought): You're always right in the middle of an important game. Get to bed! Now!

Child: Sh-t! You made me mess up my game!

Parent: I messed up your game? Get your butt in gear before I mess up something else!

Child: *(Kaboom)*

As this dialogue suggests, if you respond to a child who's having difficulty separating affect by imposing your will more intensively and "teaching him who's the boss," you probably won't help him manage his emotions and think rationally in the midst of frustration. Quite the opposite, in fact. So we often tell explosive children and their parents and teachers that there are only two goals: Goal number two: *Think clearly in the midst of frustration.* Goal number one: *Stay calm enough to achieve goal number two.*

LANGUAGE PROCESSING SKILLS

How might lagging language processing skills set the stage for a child to have a learning disability in the domains of flexibility and frustration tolerance? Most of the thinking and communicating we humans do involves language. Indeed, language is what separates humans from other species. For example, dogs don't have language. So if you were to step on a dog's tail, he'd have only three options: bark at you, bite you, or run away. But if you step on the metaphoric tail of a linguistically compromised human being, he'd have only the same three options: bark at you, bite you, or run away. From this perspective, swearing can be thought of as nothing more or less than the human "bark." It's what we humans do when we can't think of a more articulate way to express ourselves.

Many prominent theorists have underscored the importance of language skills in helping us humans reflect, self-regulate, set goals, and manage emotions. Let's examine the role of three specific language skills—*categorizing and expressing emotions, identifying and articulating one's needs,* and *solving problems*—to elucidate why this might be.

Many explosive children don't have a basic vocabulary for categorizing and expressing their emotions. This is a big problem, for it's actually very useful to be able to let people know you're "frustrated" when you're frustrated. Can you imagine feeling all the sensations associated with frustration—hot-faced, agitated, tense, explosive, and so on—without being able to let people know what you're feeling? Under such circumstances, there's some reasonable chance that words other than "frustrated" will come out of your mouth. ("Screw you," "I hate you," "Shut up," and "Leave me alone" are some of the milder possibilities.) Worse, if you don't have the word "frustrated" in your vocabulary, there's a pretty surefire chance that people are going to think you're something else ("angry," "hostile," "out-of-control," "scary"). Then they're going to treat you as if you're angry, hostile, out-of-control, or scary, and you're going to get even more frustrated.

Some children do just fine at categorizing and labeling their feelings but have trouble coming up with the words to tell you what's the matter or what they need. For example, most eighteen-month-old children don't yet have the skills to tell us what they need using words. So when they need something, they point, grunt, cry, or babble. Then we get to try to figure out what they're trying to "say." I'm hungry? My diaper's wet? Can you play with me? I'm tired? But there are many older children (and adults) whose skills at telling people what's the matter or what they need are not significantly greater than the average eighteen-month-old. That's frustrating!

Finally, language is the mechanism by which most people solve problems. That's because a lot (if not most) of the thinking we do in solving problems is in the form of language. And also because most of the solutions we have stored in our brains (from problems we've solved or seen solved previously) are in the form of language as well. (We humans aren't quite as creative as we think we are in the problem-solving department: We rely almost exclusively on past experience to help us solve problems in the present.) For example, if you find you have a flat tire, you don't have to do a whole lot of original thinking to solve the problem. You just have to think about how you (or those you've observed) have solved that problem previously. There aren't that many possibilities. You could fix the tire yourself, call your significant other, ask someone for help, call a service station, swear, cry, or leave the car for junk (some of those solutions would be more effective at solving the problem than others). The process of accessing previous solutions tends to be automatic and efficient for many children. But children whose language skills are lagging may have difficulty efficiently accessing past solutions that are stored in language. Take George, for example:

Therapist: George, I understand you got pretty frustrated at soccer the other day.

George: Yep.

Therapist: What happened?

George: The coach took me out of the game, and I didn't want to come out.

Therapist: I understand you told him you were very mad.

George: Yep.

Therapist: I think it's probably good that you told him. What did you do next?

George: He wouldn't put me back in, so I kicked him.

Therapist: You kicked the coach?

George: Yep.

Therapist: What happened next?

George: He kicked me off the team.

Therapist: I'm sorry to hear that.

George: I didn't even kick him that hard.

Therapist: I guess it wasn't important how hard you kicked him. I'm just wondering if you can think of something else you could have done when you were mad besides kick the coach.

George: Well, I didn't think of anything else then.

Therapist: Can you think of anything else now?

George: I could have asked him when he was going to put me back in.

Therapist: That probably would have been better than kicking him, yes?

George: Yes.

Therapist: How come you couldn't think of anything besides kicking him when you were at the soccer game?

George: I don't know.

Can children be taught to use a basic feeling vocabulary? To articulate their needs and frustrations more effectively? To access the more adaptive solutions that are stored in their brains more readily? Of course. But not with a reward and punishment program.

EMOTION REGULATION SKILLS

Most children (like the rest of us) are a little irritable, agitated, grumpy, cranky, grouchy, and fatigued some of the time. At these times, children (like the rest of us) tend to be less flexible and more easily frustrated. If they're lucky, the irritable mood is relatively short-lived and they return fairly quickly to their relatively happy baseline. But there are some children who are in an irritable, agitated, cranky, fatigued mood a whole lot more often than others, and they experience these feelings a whole lot more intensely. These kids' capacities for frustration tolerance and flexibility are compromised much more often, and as a result, they may fail to acquire developmentally appropriate skills for handling demands for flexibility and frustration tolerance.

Are these children depressed? Some mental health professionals reserve the term *depression* for children who are routinely blue, morose, sad, and hopeless, which actually tends not to be the case for many irritable explosive children. Do these children have bipolar disorder? Over the past five years or so, there has developed a troubling tendency for some mental health professionals to equate "explosive" and "bipolar," to interpret irritability as a purely biological entity, and to believe that a poor response to stimulant medication or antidepressants certifies a child as bipolar. This probably helps explain both the increased rates at which bipolar disorder is being diagnosed in children and the popularity of mood-stabilizing and atypical antipsychotic medications.

As you now know, there are many factors that could set the stage for a child to be explosive; irritability is only one. And there are many factors that could set the stage for a child to be irritable; brain chemistry is only one. Some children are irritable because of chronic problems—school failure, poor peer relations, being bullied—that have never been solved. Medicine doesn't fix school failure, poor peer relations, or being bullied. There are many "bipolar" children whose explosiveness is far better explained by lagging cognitive skills and whose difficulties are therefore not well addressed by the multiple mood-stabilizing medications they have been prescribed. If the only time a child looks as if he has bipolar disorder is when he's frustrated, that's not bipolar disorder; that's a learning disability in the domains of flexibility and frustration tolerance.

What's crystal clear is that the explosiveness of many children is being fueled by a fairly chronic state of irritability and agitation that makes it hard for them to respond to life's routine frustrations in an adaptive, rational manner.

Mother: Mickey, why so grumpy? It's a beautiful day outside. Why are you indoors?

Mickey (slumped in a chair, agitated): It's windy.

Mother: It's windy?

Mickey (more agitated): I said it's windy. I hate wind.

Mother: Mickey, you could be out playing basketball, swimming . . . you're this upset over a little wind?

Mickey (very agitated): It's too windy, dammit! Leave me alone!

Anxiety falls under the "emotion regulation skills" category as well because, similar to irritability, anxiety has the potential to make rational thought much more difficult. Of course, it's when we're anxious about something—a monster under the bed, an upcoming test, a new or unpredictable situation—that clear thinking is most crucial. This combination of anxiety and irrationality causes some children (the lucky ones) to cry. But a substantial number of them (the unlucky ones) explode. (The cryers are the lucky ones because we adults tend to take things far less personally and respond far more empathically to children who cry than we do to children who explode, even though the two behaviors often emanate from the same source.) Also, it seems pretty clear that many obsessive-compulsive children begin ritualizing because, in the absence of rational thought, the rituals are the only things they can come up with to reduce their anxiety.

Let's use me as an example. I used to be flight-anxious . . . that's right, scared of flying. No, I wasn't intentionally being anxious (sweaty palms, racing heart, catastrophic thoughts) so flight attendants would pay attention to me. I was truly unnerved to find myself five miles above the earth going five hundred miles per hour in an aluminum apparatus filled with gasoline, with my life in the hands of people (the pilots and air traffic controllers) I'd never met. To control this anxiety, I used to engage in a few important rituals to ensure the safe progress of my flight: I had to sit in a window seat (so I could scan the skies for oncoming aircraft), and had to review the emergency instruction card before the plane took off. I knew these rituals worked because all the flights I'd been on had delivered me safely to my destination.

Did these rituals cause me to behave oddly at times? On one flight, my plane was cruising along at thirty-three thousand feet or so and I was, as usual, vigilantly scanning the horizon for threatening aircraft. Then the unthinkable happened: I spotted an aircraft far off on the horizon ascending in the general direction of my airplane. By my expert calculation, we had about five minutes before the paths of the two planes crossed and my life would come to an abrupt, fiery end. So I did what any very anxious, increasingly irrational, human being would do: I rang for the flight attendant. There was no time to spare.

"Do you see that airplane down there?" I sputtered, pointing toward the speck many miles off in the distance. She peered out the window. "Do you think the captain knows it's there?" I demanded.

The flight attendant tried to hide her amusement (or amazement, I wasn't sure which) and said, "I'll be sure to let him know."

I was greatly relieved, albeit certain that my heroism was not fully appreciated by either the flight attendant or the passengers seated near me (who were now scanning the aircraft for empty seats to move to). The plane landed safely, of course, and as I was leaving the airplane once we'd landed, the flight attendant and pilot were waiting at the door and smiled as I approached. The flight attendant tugged on the pilot's sleeve and introduced me: "Captain, this is the gentleman who was helping you fly the plane."

I'm proud to say that although I still generally prefer window seats, I no longer scan the skies for oncoming aircraft or review the emergency manual (and have survived hundreds of flights on which I did neither). How did I get over my flight anxiety? Experience. And by thinking (clearly). An Air Florida pilot got the process going. As I was boarding this Air Florida flight, the captain was greeting passengers at the door of the aircraft. I seized the opportunity.

"You're going to fly the plane safely, aren't you?" I sputtered.

The pilot's response was more helpful than he knew: "What, you think I want to die, buddy?"

That the pilot wasn't particularly enthusiastic about dying was an important revelation, and it got me thinking. About the thousands of planes in the air across the world at any given time and the slim odds of something disastrous happening to the plane that I was on. About the millions of flights that arrive at their destinations uneventfully each year. About the many, many flights I have been on that arrived safely. About how calm the flight attendants look. About how many of my fellow passengers are fast asleep. Even when there's turbulence. Quite unintentionally, that Air Florida pilot had given me a new way of thinking, which was helpful to me during moments when I was inclined to become highly irrational. Instead of staring out the window thinking "What if the wing falls off?" I could instead think a less anxiety-provoking thought, such as, "The pilot doesn't want to die" or "The likelihood of something catastrophic happening to my aircraft is really quite slim." As you'll see, one of the most valuable things we can do for an explosive child is to help him stay rational at times when he's likely to become irrational.

Can irritable or anxious children be helped to problem solve more adaptively and at the same time reduce their irritability and anxiety? Certainly. But not by putting a lot of effort into coming up with new and creative ways to punish them.

COGNITIVE FLEXIBILITY SKILLS

Very young children tend to be fairly rigid, black-and-white, literal, inflexible thinkers. That's because they're still making sense of the world and it's easier to put two and two together if you don't have to worry about exceptions to the rule or alternative ways of looking at things. As children develop, they learn that, in fact, most things in life are "gray": There *are* exceptions to the rule and alternative ways of interpreting things. We don't go home from Grandma's house the same way every time; we don't eat dinner at the exact same time every day; and the weather doesn't always cooperate with our plans. Unfortunately, for some children, gray thinking doesn't develop as readily as we might wish. Though they are often diagnosed with disorders such as nonverbal learning disability or Asperger's disorder, these children can best be thought of as "black-and-white thinkers stuck in a gray world." They often have significant difficulty approaching the world in a flexible, adaptable way and become extremely frustrated when events don't proceed as they had originally configured.

More specifically, these children often have a strong preference for predictability and routines, and struggle when events are unpredictable, uncertain, and ambiguous. These are the kids who run into trouble when they need to adjust or reconfigure their expectations, tend to overfocus on facts and details, and often have trouble recognizing the obvious or "seeing the big picture." In practical terms, this is the child who may insist on going out for recess at a certain time on a given day because it is the time the class "always goes out" for recess, failing to take into account both the likely consequences of insisting on the original plan of action (e.g., being at recess alone) and important conditions (an assembly, perhaps) that would suggest the need for an adaptation in plan. These children may experience enormous frustration as they struggle to apply concrete rules to a world where few such rules apply:

Child (in a car): Dad, this isn't the way we usually go home.

Father (driving): I thought we'd go a different way this time, just for a change of pace.

Child: But this isn't the right way!

Father: I know this isn't the way we usually go, but it may even be faster.

Child: We can't go this way! It's not the same! I don't know this way!

Father: Look, it's not that big a deal to go a different way every once in a while.

Child: *(Kaboom)*

If you're guessing that Jennifer (star of the waffle episode in chapter 1) was a black-and-white thinker stuck in a gray world, you'd be right. Can the Jennifers of the world be helped to approach the world in a more flexible manner? You bet. But not if the adults around them are busy being inflexible themselves.

SOCIAL SKILLS

There are few human activities that require more flexibility, complex thinking, and rapid processing than social interactions. Researchers have delineated a set of specific thinking skills—known as social information processing skills—that come into play in practically all social interactions. A brief review of these thinking skills will help you understand just how frustrating social interactions can be, especially for children who aren't good at them, and how lagging social skills can set the stage for explosions.

Let's say a boy is standing in a hallway at school and a peer comes up and, with a big smile on his face, whacks the boy hard on the back and says, "Hi!" The boy who was whacked on the back now has a split second to attend to and try to pick up on the important qualities of the social cues of this situation ("Who just whacked me on the back? Aside from the person's smile, is there anything about his posture or facial expression or this context that tells me whether this was a friendly or unfriendly smile and whack?"). At the same time he must connect those cues with his previous experiences ("When have other people, and this person in particular, whacked me on the back and smiled at me before?") in order to interpret the cue ("Was this an overexuberant greeting or an aggressive act?"). Then he has to think about what he wants to have happen next

("That was a mean thing to do . . . I'd like to avoid getting into a fight with this person" or "That was a nice greeting . . . I'd like to play a game with him"). Then, on the basis of his interpretation of the cue and the outcome he desires, the boy must begin to think about how to respond, either by remembering his experiences in similar situations or by thinking of new responses. Then, he must evaluate the different possible responses, consider the likely outcomes of each ("If I smile back, he'll probably ask me to play a game with him"), choose a response, enact it, monitor the course of events throughout, and adjust the response accordingly.

Sounds like a lot of thinking for one event, yes? The key point is that this process is nonstop and requires a lot of efficiency and flexibility. It's barely noticeable to people for whom it happens automatically, but it's very frustrating if you're not one of those people.

Many explosive children have trouble attending to appropriate social cues and nuances; do not accurately interpret those cues ("He hates me," "Everybody's out to get me," "No one likes me"); are inefficient at connecting cues with past experience; may not be very efficient at considering how they want a social interaction to ensue; may have a limited repertoire of responses and end up applying the identical responses (giggling, poking, intruding) to situations in which such responses are inappropriate; may be quite unskilled at recognizing how they're coming across or appreciating how their behavior is affecting others; and may lack the skills for handling the most basic of social interactions (starting a conversation, entering a group, sharing). Such children—who suffer from what Daniel Goleman has referred to as emotional illiteracy—are likely to find social interactions extremely frustrating. This can, at the least, contribute to the child's general level of frustration; at worst, it may lead to a chronic pattern of explosions.

Can these children be helped to develop more adaptive social skills? Yes, usually. It does take a while. But only if adults recognize that trying hard to motivate a child who's already motivated to do well wouldn't be the best way to go about teaching the social skills that are lacking.

Just in case you were wondering, children are often deficient in skills that cut across multiple pathways. Perhaps the most important thing the pathways can help us understand is that flexibility and frustration tolerance are not skills that come naturally to all children. We tend to think that all children are created equal in these capacities, and this tendency causes many adults to believe that explosive children must not *want* to be compliant and handle frustration in an adaptable way. As you now know, in most cases this simply isn't true.

By the way, there's a big difference between interpreting the pathways described in this chapter as "excuses" rather than as "explanations." When the pathways are invoked as excuses, the door slams shut on the process of thinking about how to help a child. Conversely, when the pathways are used as explanations for a child's behavior, the door to helping swings wide open, for the pathways provide us with an improved understanding of the child's needs and a clearer sense of what we need to do next. It's very difficult to be helpful without this comprehensive, in-depth understanding of a child's difficulties.

TRIGGERS

There's one other piece of terminology to cover before the chapter ends: *triggers*.

What's a trigger? A situation or event that routinely precipitates explosive outbursts. Triggers can best be thought of as *problems that have yet to be solved*. The possibilities are endless, but here's the short list: homework, sensory hypersensitivities, tics, sibling interactions, bedtime, waking up in the morning, meals, being bored, riding in the car, recess, being teased, reading, writing, being tired, being hot, or being hungry.

So while the pathways are what set the stage for a child to be explosive (skills that need to be trained), triggers are the situations or events over which the child is actually exploding. Help the child develop the thinking skills and solve the problems and there won't be any more explosions.

Once you know what your child's pathways and triggers are, his explosions become highly predictable. Lots of folks believe that a child's explosions are unpredictable and occur "out of the blue," but that theory is seldom substantiated. For reasons that will become much clearer in Chapter 6, predictable explosions are a lot easier to deal with than unpredictable ones.

4

Pathways and Triggers Brought to Life

As you might imagine—given the different pathways and triggers that could be involved with each individual child—inflexibility and poor frustration tolerance can look different in different children. So that the characteristics you've read about start to come to life, it's useful for you to have a good idea of what they look like in other kids. You'll probably see similarities between the children described in this chapter and the explosive child you're trying to parent or teach. These children and their families are revisited in one way or another throughout the book.

CASEY

Casey was a six-year-old boy who lived with his parents and younger sister. His parents reported that, at home, Casey was very hyperactive, had difficulty playing by himself (but wasn't great at playing with other kids, either), and had a lot of difficulty with transitions (getting him to come indoors after playing outside was often a major ordeal). His parents also reported that Casey seemed to be quite bright, in that he had excellent memory for factual information, but that he became anxious when presented with new tasks or situations and was frequently in an irritable, agitated mood. The parents had read a lot about ADHD; while they thought that this diagnosis fit Casey, they felt that many of his difficulties fell outside the realm of this disorder. They thought the term "control freak" fit their son better than any traditional diagnosis. Casey was quite restricted and rigid in the clothes he was willing to wear and the food he was willing to eat (he often complained that certain fabrics were annoying to him and that many common foods "smelled funny"). Most of these characteristics had been present since Casey was a toddler.

His parents had previously consulted a psychologist, who helped them establish a reward and punishment program. The parents vigilantly implemented the program but found that Casey's hyperactivity, inflexibility, and irritability were more potent than his clear desire to obtain rewards and avoid punishments. Indeed, the program actually seemed to frustrate him further, but the psychologist encouraged the parents to stick with it, certain that Casey's behavior would improve. It didn't, so the parents discontinued the program after about three months. They often tried to talk to Casey about his behavior, but even when he was in a good mood, his capacity for thinking about his own behavior seemed limited; after a few seconds, he would yell "I can't talk about this right now!" and run out of the room.

Casey had difficulties at school, too. His first-grade teacher reported that Casey would occasionally hit or yell at other children during less structured activities, particularly when he did not get his way. Like the parents, Casey's teacher was impressed by his factual knowledge but concerned by his poor problem-solving skills. When lessons called for recall of rote information, Casey was the star of the class. When lessons required the application of this information to more abstract, complex, real-life situations, his responses were disorganized and off the mark. When he was frustrated by a particular classroom situation or task, he would yell "I can't do this!" and would become quite agitated or start crying; sometimes he would run out of the classroom. On several occasions, he ran out of the school, which caused great concern for his safety. Sometimes he regained his composure quickly; other times it took twenty to thirty minutes for him to calm down. Afterward, Casey was either remorseful ("I'm sorry I ran out of the classroom . . . I know I shouldn't do that") or had difficulty remembering the episode altogether.

Casey's teacher reported that she could often tell from the moment Casey walked through the door in the morning that he was going to have a tough day. But she also observed that Casey was capable of falling apart even when his day seemed to be going smoothly. The teacher was becoming increasingly concerned about Casey's relationships with other children; Casey seemed to lack an appreciation for the impact of his actions on others and seemed unable to use the feedback he received from others to adjust his behavior.

In Casey's first session with a new therapist, he was very hyperactive and seemed unwilling or unable to talk about the important problems that he might need help with. He bounced from one toy to another in the therapist's office. When his parents were brought into the session, he settled down just long enough to hear that the reason he had been brought to another psychologist was that he sometimes became upset when things didn't go exactly the way he thought they would. He agreed that this was sometimes a problem. When the parents tried to get Casey to talk about this issue, he buried his face in his mother's shoulder; when the parents persisted, he warned, "I can't talk about this right now!" When they persisted further, he became red-faced and agitated and ran out of the office.

"Was that pretty typical?" the therapist asked the parents.

"No, at home he'd have become a lot more frustrated," replied his mother. "He doesn't usually hit us—although he has hit kids at school—but he falls apart completely . . . turns red, screams or cries, yells 'I hate you!' "

"You know, in some ways his running out of the room is adaptive," the therapist commented.

"How's that?" asked the father, a little surprised.

"Well, based on what you've told me, it seems pretty clear that he has a lot of trouble thinking and talking about his own behavior and tolerating the frustration he feels when we ask him to do those things," the therapist said. "While we wish he would 'use his words' to discuss things with us, his running out of the room probably keeps him from doing other things—swearing, throwing things, becoming physically threatening—that would be a lot worse."

"We can live with a lot of Casey's behaviors," said his mother. "But his explosions . . . and the way they disrupt our entire family . . . and our concern about what's going to happen to him if we don't help him . . . really worry us."

What were Casey's pathways? So far, it seems reasonable to hypothesize that difficulty shifting cognitive set (executive), irritability (emotion regulation), discomfort with new tasks or situations (cognitive flexibility), and possibly social difficulties were setting the stage for his explosions. Whether Casey's difficulty talking about his problems reflected lagging language processing skills wasn't yet clear. In terms of triggers, sensory hypersensitivities certainly seemed to be coming into play.

Thus, the initial goal was to achieve greater certainty on Casey's pathways (so as to identify skills that he needed to learn) and to develop a comprehensive list of triggers (in order to identify the specific problems that needed to be solved). Whether medications for reducing hyperactivity and impulsivity and reducing irritability might be necessary wasn't yet certain.

HELEN

Helen and her mother and father first sought help for her explosions when she was seven years old. Helen was described as a charming, sensitive, creative, energetic, sociable girl. Her parents also described her as intense, easily angered, argumentative, resistant, and downright nasty when frustrated. They had observed that Helen seemed to have a lot of trouble making the transition from one activity to another and tended to fall apart when things didn't go exactly as she had anticipated. They reported that weekends were especially difficult; although Helen didn't love going to school, she became bored during unstructured weekend time and became very difficult to please. Helen's piano teacher observed that Helen tended to become easily frustrated and often balked at trying new pieces of music. Her second-grade teacher reported that Helen had a tendency to grumble when new lessons were introduced. Psychoeducational testing indicated that while Helen was above-average in intelligence, her expressive language skills were delayed. (If you're thinking, based on the above information, that the language and cognitive flexibility pathways might be coming into play, you may be on to something!)

In one of their early meetings with Helen's therapist, her parents recounted one of her explosions during the previous week.

"On Tuesday, Helen told me she'd like to have chili for dinner the next night," recalled her father. "So, on Wednesday afternoon, I left work a little early and made her the chili she had asked for. When she got home from swimming late Wednesday afternoon, she seemed a little tired; when I announced to her that I had made her the chili she wanted, she grumbled, 'I want macaroni and cheese.' This took me a little bit by surprise, since I know she really loves chili. It was also a little irritating, since I had put time into doing something nice for her. So I told her she would have to eat the chili. But she seemed unable to get macaroni and cheese out of her head, and I continued to insist that she eat the chili for dinner. The more I insisted, the more she fell apart.

Eventually, she lost it completely. She was screaming and crying, but I was determined that she would eat the chili I had made her."

"What did you do then?" the therapist asked.

"We sent her to her bedroom and told her she had to stay there until she was ready to eat the chili," said Helen's mother. "For the next hour she screamed and cried in her room; at one point, she was banging on her mirror and broke it. Can you imagine? All this over chili! I went up to her room a few times to see if I could calm her down, but it was impossible. Helen was totally irrational. The amazing thing is that, at one point, she couldn't even remember what she was upset about."

"Why was it so important to you that she eat the chili instead of the macaroni and cheese?" the therapist asked.

"Because I inconvenienced myself to do something nice for her," the father responded.

"Sounds like a legitimate concern to me," the therapist said. "Do you think that your enduring this explosion—having Helen go nuts in her room for an hour, breaking her mirror, and ruining your evening—made it any less likely that she'll explode the next time she's frustrated over something similar?" the therapist asked.

"No" was the instantaneous, unanimous response.

"What was Helen like when the episode was all over?" the therapist asked.

"Very remorseful and very loving," the mother responded. "It's hard to know whether to reciprocate her affection or to hold a grudge for a while to cement the point that we don't like that kind of behavior."

"Well," the therapist replied, "if you don't think that inducing and enduring explosions is going to help her deal better with frustration the next time, then it follows that holding a grudge probably isn't going to help either."

"Yes, but how will she learn that that kind of behavior is unacceptable?" asked the mother.

"From what I can gather," the therapist said, "the fact that you disapprove of that kind of behavior is pretty well cemented in her mind already . . . so I doubt that we'll be needing more cement. She also seems genuinely motivated to please you both . . . and seems as unhappy about her explosions as you are . . . so I'm not sure she needs additional motivation." What Helen and her parents did need was a different way to resolve disagreements and problems.

"We've got some skills to teach Helen," the therapist continued. "We need to help her deal better with uncertainty and unpredictability, and it sounds like we might have some language skills to teach her as well. I also want to get a much better sense about the precise situations that are causing a lot of explosions. Then we'll know what problems we need to solve. I'd like you to do me a favor. Make me a list during the coming week of all the situations in which Helen became frustrated. My bet is that there are probably seven or eight 'triggers' accounting for most of her explosions. The list will help me know what those are."

DANNY

Danny was a fifth grader whose mother and father had divorced amicably when Danny was seven and still considered themselves "co-parents." Danny and his younger sister stayed with the father and his fiancée every weekend. The mother described Danny as very bright, perfectionistic, moody, irritable, and, as fate would have it, very easily frustrated. The mother was especially concerned about Danny's "rage attacks," which had occurred several times a week since Danny was a toddler. During such episodes, he would become verbally abusive and physically aggressive. The mother was also worried about how these attacks were affecting Danny's sister, who, at times, seemed scared of her older brother and, at other times, seemed to take some pleasure in provoking him. Danny had never had a rage attack at school.

He had seen numerous mental health professionals over the years; like many explosive kids, Danny accumulated a fairly impressive number of psychiatric diagnoses, including oppositional-defiant disorder, depression, and bipolar disorder. His family physician had medicated

Danny with Ritalin several years previously, but Danny had remained moody, rigid, and explosive. A psychiatrist had subsequently prescribed an antidepressant, but this medication caused Danny to become significantly more agitated and hyperactive.

"Danny can be in what seems to be a perfectly pleasant mood and then—bang!—something doesn't go quite the way he thought it would, and he's cursing and hitting," his mother reported. "I don't know what to do. The other day he and I were in the car together and I took a wrong turn. Danny suddenly became very agitated that it was taking us longer to get where we were going than it should have. All of a sudden, I had a ten-year-old kid punching me! In the car! While I'm driving! It's insanity!

"I'm tired of people telling me this behavior is occurring because I'm a single parent. My ex-husband is still very much involved in Danny's life, and there hasn't been any of the back stabbing that takes place with some divorces. I will say I think his dad tries too hard to be Danny's best friend. Anyway, these explosions started way before there were problems in our marriage, although, I must admit, he's a lot more explosive when he's with me than he is when he's with his father."

In conversations with his new therapist, Danny seemed genuinely contrite over the behavior his mother had described. He said he'd been trying very hard not to be physically or verbally aggressive but didn't seem to be able to help himself. The therapist's sense early on was that Danny's extreme irritability was a major factor contributing to his explosions; there was also some suggestion that black-and-white thinking (the cognitive flexibility pathway) might be coming into play. He said he exploded more with his mother because she "nags too much."

At the beginning of one session, the mother described Danny's biggest explosion of the week.

"Yesterday, I told him he had to come in from playing basketball to eat dinner. He whined a little, but I insisted. Next thing I know, his face is red, he's calling me every name in the book, he's accusing me of ruining his life, and I'm hiding behind a door trying to shield myself from getting kicked. I was petrified. So was his sister. And it's not the first time. Twenty minutes later, he was sorry. But this is just ridiculous," said the mother. "I'm sick of being hit, and it's just impossible to reason with him once he gets going."

"What did you do once he'd calmed down?" the therapist asked.

"I punished him for swearing at me and trying to kick me," replied the mother. "I feel he needs to be disciplined for that kind of behavior."

"I can understand you feeling that way. Tell me, have you always punished him when he's acted like that?" the therapist asked.

"You bet," the mother said. "I'm not willing to just let that kind of disrespect slide."

"What happens when you punish him?" the therapist asked.

"He goes nuts," she said. "It's horrible."

"But despite all the punishing, he's still very verbally and physically aggressive, yes?"

"That's why I'm here," the mother said, smiling through gritted teeth.

"Well," the therapist said, "I'm all in favor of punishment when it's productive—you know, when it's effective at changing a child's behavior. But I'm not real keen on punishment just for the sake of punishment."

"What, I should let him get away with what he does?" demanded the mother.

"Don't get me wrong," the therapist said. "We need to help him stop exploding and hitting. But based on what you've been telling me, 'not letting him get away with it' hasn't changed his behavior at all."

The mother pondered this observation for a moment.

"I think I figured that eventually the message would get through if I just kept plugging away," she explained. "I never stopped to think that maybe the message would never get through."

"Oh, I suspect Danny knows you don't like his behavior," the therapist said. "In fact, I'm reasonably certain he even knows how you'd like him to behave."

"Then why doesn't he?" the mother demanded.

"Now that I've met with Danny a few times, I get the

feeling he's generally in a pretty cranky mood. I know he's not crazy about coming here, but is that his mood most of the time?" the therapist asked.

"Absolutely," replied the mother. "We call him Grumpy. He doesn't seem to enjoy himself very much . . . and he's very uptight. Everything seems to bother him."

"What an unpleasant existence," the therapist said. "And it has very unpleasant implications for everyone around him."

"You can say that again," the mother sighed. "But what does that have to do with his being explosive and angry and trying to hurt me?"

"Well, if we view him as grumpy and irritable, rather than as disrespectful and oppositional, then I think our approach to dealing with him might look a lot different," the therapist said.

"I don't understand what you mean," said the mother.

"What I mean is that kids who are grumpy and irritable often don't need more discipline," the therapist said. "I've yet to see discipline be especially useful at helping a kid be less irritable and agitated."

"I still don't understand how being irritable is an excuse for his being so disrespectful and angry toward me," said the mother.

"Well, it's more of an explanation than an excuse," the therapist replied. "But when people go through the day in an irritable, cranky mood, they experience every request or change or inconvenience as yet another demand for an expenditure of energy. If you think about it, over the course of a day or week, a person's energy for dealing with these requests and changes and inconveniences starts to wane. Often the event that sends an irritable, cranky person over the edge isn't necessarily the biggest; rather, it's the one that happened after he'd expended his last ounce of energy.

"Think of times you've been tired after a long day at work," the therapist continued. "Those are probably the times when you're least adaptable and least flexible and when very minor things are likely to set you off. I think Danny is in that state of mind fairly continuously."

"There's no way I'm going to tell him he's allowed to hit me just because he's irritable," said the mother.

"Oh, I'm not saying you should allow him to hit you," the therapist said. "The hitting has got to stop. But to get the hitting and swearing and tantrums to stop, I think we need to focus on things you can do before he explodes, rather than on what you can do after he's exploded. And we need to focus on all the ingredients that are fueling his inflexibility and explosiveness. From what I've seen so far, helping him with his irritability will be high on the list."

MITCHELL

Mitchell was dragged into yet another therapist's office for an initial appointment when he was a fifteen-year-old ninth grader. The therapist met first with Mitchell's mother, a law professor, and father, a practicing lawyer, and was told that Mitchell had been diagnosed with both Tourette's disorder and bipolar disorder but was refusing all medication except an antihypertensive, which he was taking to control his tics. The therapist was also told that Mitchell was extremely unhappy about having been brought to his office that day, for he greatly distrusted mental health professionals. The parents reported that Mitchell was extremely irritable (emotion regulation pathway?), had no friends (social skills pathway?), and became frustrated at the drop of a hat. But, aside from pathways, a key to understanding Mitchell's difficulties was watching him interact with his parents.

The parents reported that Mitchell, their youngest child (the others were already living away from home), was extremely bright and very eccentric, but he was repeating the ninth grade because of a very rough time he'd had at a local prep school the year before.

"This is a classic case of wasted potential," said the father. "We were devastated by what happened last year."

"What happened?" the therapist asked.

"He just plain bombed out of prep school," said the

father. "Here's a kid with an IQ in the 140s, and he's not making it at one of the area's top prep schools. He practically had a nervous breakdown over it. He had to be hospitalized for a week because he tried to slit his wrist."

"That sounds very serious and very scary. How is he now?" the therapist asked.

"Lousy," said the mother. "He has no self-esteem left . . . he's lost all faith in himself. And he doesn't seem to be able to complete any schoolwork at all anymore. We think he's depressed."

"Where's he going to school now?" the therapist asked.

"Our local high school," the mother replied. "They're very nice there and everything, but we don't think he's being challenged by the work, bright as he is."

"Of course, there's more to doing well in school besides smarts," the therapist said. "Can I take a look at the testing you had done?"

The parents gave the therapist a copy of a psychoeducational evaluation that had been performed when Mitchell was in the seventh grade. The report documented a twenty-five-point discrepancy between his exceptional verbal skills and average nonverbal skills, difficulty on tasks sensitive to distractibility, very slow processing speed, and below-average written language skills. But the examiner had concluded that Mitchell had no difficulties that would interfere with his learning.

"This is an interesting report," the therapist said.

"How's that?" asked the father.

"Well, it may give us some clues as to why Mitchell might be struggling to live up to everyone's expectations in school," the therapist said.

"We were told he had no learning problems," the mother said.

"I think that was probably inaccurate," the therapist said. He then explained the potential ramifications of some of the evaluation findings. As they talked, it became clearer that Mitchell was indeed struggling most on tasks involving a lot of writing, problem solving, rapid processing, and sustained effort. "That's something we're going to have to take a closer look at," the therapist said.

"Of course, he's still very bright," said the father.

"There are some areas in which he is clearly quite bright," the therapist said. "And some areas that may be making it very hard for him to show how bright he is. My bet is that he finds that disparity quite frustrating."

"Oh, he's frustrated, all right," said the mother. "We all are."

After a while, Mitchell was invited to come into the office. He refused to meet with the therapist alone, so his parents remained in the room.

"I'm sick of mental health professionals," Mitchell announced from the outset.

"How come?" the therapist asked.

"Never had much use for them . . . none of them has ever done me any good," Mitchell answered.

"Don't be rude, Mitchell," his father intoned.

"SHUT UP, FATHER!" Mitchell boomed. "HE WASN'T TALKING TO YOU!"

The storm passed quickly. "It sounds like you've been through quite a bit in the past two years," the therapist said.

"WHAT DID YOU TELL HIM?!" Mitchell boomed at his parents.

"We told him about the trouble you had in prep school," the mother answered, "and about your being suicidal, and about how we don't . . ."

"ENOUGH!" Mitchell screamed. "I don't know this man from Adam, and you've already told him my life story! And I wouldn't have been suicidal if I hadn't been on about eighty-seven different medications at the time!"

"What were you taking back then?" the therapist asked.

"I don't know," Mitchell said, rubbing hard on his forehead. "You tell him, Mother!"

"I think he's been on about every psychiatric drug known to mankind," said the mother. "Lithium, Prozac . . ."

"STOP EXAGGERATING, MOTHER!" Mitchell boomed.

"Mitchell, don't be rude to your mother," said the father.

"If you don't stop telling me not to be rude, I'm leaving!" Mitchell screamed.

Once again, the storm quickly subsided. "What medicines are you taking now?" the therapist asked.

"Just something for my tics," Mitchell replied. "And don't even think about telling me to take something else! Let's just get off this topic!"

"He doesn't even take his tic medication all the time," said the mother. "That's why he still tics so much."

"MOTHER, STOP!" Mitchell boomed. "I don't care about the tics! Leave me alone about them!"

"It's just that . . ." the mother began speaking again.

"MOTHER, NO!" Mitchell boomed. His mother stopped.

"Mitchell, are you suicidal now?" the therapist asked.

"NO! And if you ask me that again, I'm leaving!"

"He still doesn't feel very good about himself, though," the father said.

"I FEEL JUST FINE!" Mitchell boomed. "You're the ones who need a psychologist, not me!" Mitchell turned to the therapist. "Can you do something about them?" The father chuckled at this question.

"WHAT'S SO FUNNY?!" Mitchell boomed.

"If I might interrupt," the therapist said, "I know you didn't want to be here today, and I can understand why you might not have much faith in yet another mental health professional. But I'm interested . . . what is it you'd like me to do about your parents?"

"Tell them to leave me alone," he growled. "I'm fine."

"Yes, he's got everything under complete control," the father said sarcastically.

"PLEASE!" Mitchell boomed.

"If I told them to leave you alone, do you think they would?" the therapist asked.

"No." He glared at his parents. "I don't."

"Is it fair," the therapist said, speaking carefully, "to say that your interactions with your parents are very frustrating for you?"

Mitchell turned to his parents. "You've found another genius," he said. "We need to pay money and waste our time on this guy telling us the obvious?"

"Mitchell!" said the father. "Don't be rude!"

"STOP TELLING ME WHAT TO DO!" Mitchell boomed.

"I appreciate your looking out for me," the therapist said to the father. "But I actually want to hear what Mitchell has to say." The therapist looked back at Mitchell. "I don't think I can get them to leave you alone without you being here."

"I don't think you can get them to leave me alone *with* me being here," Mitchell said. Then he paused for a moment. "How often do I have to come?" he asked.

"Well, to start, I'd like you to come every other week," the therapist said. "I'd like your parents to come every week. Is that reasonable?"

"Fine!" he said. "Can we leave now?"

"I'd like to spend a few more minutes with your parents. But you can wait outside if you'd like." Mitchell left the office.

"We've got a lot of work to do," the therapist said. "My initial impression is that Mitchell is extremely irritable, pretty black-and-white, and doesn't have a very good sense of how he's coming across. He's tried to kill himself once . . ."

"Twice," interjected the mother. "He tried twice in the same year."

"Twice," the therapist continued. "He's got very high expectations academically but some significant learning issues getting in the way; he isn't satisfactorily medicated at the moment; and he has no faith in the mental health profession. And there's a particular trigger that seems to set him off very reliably."

"What is it?" the mother asked.

"You guys," the therapist replied.

There was a long pause. Finally, the mother said, "Where do we start?"

"Well, I need more information about a lot of things," the therapist said. "But one thing is certain: We're not going to get anywhere unless I can establish a relationship with him. And we're going to have to help you guys learn how to communicate and collaborate so that Mitchell's interactions with you guys aren't so frustrating for all of you."

"Oh, would you say there's some tension in our family?" the father said sarcastically.

"A little bit," the therapist smiled.

"So we come back next week?" asked the mother.

"You do," the therapist said.

At this point you might be thinking, "Wow, I don't have it so bad" or "What, he thinks we don't know what explosions look like?" or "Can we please get on with the show here? What do I *do*?" Just remember, the most important part of what you do is to identify your child's pathways and triggers. Otherwise, you can't possibly know exactly what to do. But before we get to what you do *next*, we've got one more avenue to explore: why what you've done *already* may not have been well matched to the needs of your child.

5

The Truth About Consequences

"You know, first we thought Amy was just a willful, spoiled kid," one father recalled. "We had all these books and TV personalities and our pediatrician telling us that if we were simply firmer and more consistent with her, things would get better. Of course, Amy's grandparents added their two cents; they were constantly telling my wife and me about how Amy would have been handled in the 'good old days.' So we did the whole sticker chart and time-out routine for a long time. It makes me shudder to think of how much time that poor kid spent in time-out. But we were told the lessons we were trying to teach her would sink in eventually. Sometimes she wouldn't stay in the time-out, and she'd try to kick us and bite us when we tried to hold her there. When we'd confine her to her room, she'd become destructive. We couldn't figure out what we were doing wrong.

"So we went from doctor to doctor looking for answers. One doctor said Amy's tantrums were just her way of getting our attention and told us to ignore the tantrums and give her lots of attention for good behaviors. But ignoring her didn't help her calm down when she was frustrated about something. I don't care what the experts say, you can't just ignore your kid while she's being destructive and violent.

"Another doctor—this was around when she was eight years old—told us Amy had a lot of anger and rage. Amy spent the next year in play therapy, with this therapist trying to figure out what she was so angry about. He sort of ignored us when we told him Amy wasn't angry all the time, only when things didn't go exactly the way she thought they would. He never did figure out why she was so angry.

"The last person we went to was a child psychiatrist. We weren't all that enthusiastic about the idea, but she thought medicine might help Amy hold it together better. We figured we had nothing to lose. But when the first medicine didn't get the job done, she added another . . .

then another. Maybe there are some kids who do well on meds, but Amy wasn't one of them . . . all she had to show for all that medicine was an extra thirty pounds. In the meantime, we're still trying to figure out how to live with a kid like this.

"We've done everything we've been told to do. We've paid a big price—and I'm not just talking about money—listening to different professionals and trying strategies that weren't on target. All along we were convinced that her explosions were our fault. If it's our fault, how come our other two kids are so well behaved?"

Psychology and psychiatry are imprecise sciences, and different mental health professionals have different theories and interpretations of explosive behavior in children. As you now know, children may exhibit such behavior for any of a variety of reasons, so there's no right or wrong way to explain it and no one-size-fits-all approach to changing it. The key is to find explanations and interventions that are well matched to individual children and their families.

Probably the most recommended and widely used approach to understanding and changing the behavior of explosive children—the conventional wisdom—is what can generically be referred to as the standard behavior management approach. There are a few central beliefs associated with this approach. The first is that somewhere along the line, noncompliant children have *learned* that their tantrums, explosions, swearing, screaming, and destructiveness bring them attention or help them get their way by coercing (or convincing) their parents to "give in." This belief often gives rise to the notion that explosions are planned, intentional, purposeful, and under the child's conscious control ("He's a very manipulative kid. He knows exactly what buttons to push!"), which, in turn, often causes adults to take the behavior very personally ("Why is he doing this to me?"). As you read in Chapter 2, a corollary to the belief that such behavior is learned is that the child has been poorly taught or disciplined ("What that kid needs is parents who are willing to give him a good kick in the pants"). Parents who become convinced of this often blame themselves for their child's explosive behavior ("It must be us . . . we must be doing something wrong . . . nothing we do seems to work with this kid"). Finally, if you believe that such behavior is learned and the result of poor parenting and lax discipline, then it follows that it can also be unlearned with better and more convincing teaching and discipline.

In general, this unlearning and re-teaching process includes: (1) providing the child with lots of positive attention to reduce the desirability of negative attention; (2) teaching parents to issue fewer and clearer commands; (3) teaching the child that compliance is expected and enforced on all parental commands and that he must comply quickly because his parents are going to issue a command only once or twice; (4) implementing a record-keeping system (points, stickers, happy faces, and the like) to track the child's performance on specified target behaviors (such as complying with adult commands, doing homework, getting ready for school, brushing teeth, and so forth); (5) delivering consequences—rewards, such as allowance money and special privileges, and punishments, such as time-outs and the loss of privileges—contingent upon the child's successful or unsuccessful performance; and (6) teaching the child that his parents won't back down in the face of explosions. This conventional approach isn't magic; it merely formalizes practices that are considered important cornerstones of effective parenting: being clear about how a child should and should not behave, consistently expecting and insisting upon appropriate behavior, and giving a child the incentive to perform such behavior.

Some parents and their children benefit enormously from these programs, find that the above procedures provide some needed structure and organization to family discipline, and end up sticking with the program for a long time. Other parents may not stick with a formal behavior management program for long but still change some fundamental aspects of their approach to parenting and therefore become more effective at teaching and motivating their children. Still other parents may embark on a behavior management program with an initial burst of enthusiasm, energy, and vigilance but become less enthusiastic, energetic, and vigilant over time. These parents often return to their old, familiar patterns of parenting.

And many parents find that behavior management programs don't improve their child's behavior, even when they stick with the program. Indeed, some parents find that such programs actually *increase* the frequency and intensity of their child's explosions and cause their interactions with their child to *worsen*. Why? Because reward and punishment programs don't teach the skills of flexibility and frustration tolerance. And because getting punished or not receiving an anticipated reward makes kids more frustrated, not less. And because, as you may have noticed, being more inflexible yourself doesn't help your child be more flexible. There's a simple equation to summarize this phenomenon:

inflexibility + inflexibility = explosion

But let's go back and take a closer look at what happened when Amy's parents tried to implement behavior management procedures. First, the parents tried to give directions in a way that made it easier for Amy to comply and were encouraged to "catch Amy being good" (with verbal praise, hugs, and the like) every time she complied. Then she and her parents identified a variety of meaningful rewards that could be earned in exchange for compliance, and the parents were helped to design a "currency" system—in her case, a point system—as a way of keeping track of the percentage of times Amy complied with their requests. The points were to be exchanged periodically for the rewards, each of which had a price tag. Then the parents began implementing the time-out procedure when Amy did not comply. So Amy was receiving a specified number of points every time she complied with a parental request and was confined to time-out and lost points when she did not comply. Amy was now, most assuredly, very motivated to comply (assuming, of course, that she wasn't motivated in the first place).

The following scenario ensued. The parents would give directions. Amy, whose skills at shifting cognitive set were not outstanding and who didn't have the linguistic skills to let people know that, wouldn't comply. The parents would repeat their directive. Amy, still at a loss for words, would become frustrated, for she wasn't enthusiastic about losing points or ending up in time-out. The parents would remind her of the consequences for not obeying and of the necessity for immediate compliance. Rather than helping Amy immediately access the file in her brain that contained the critical information ("If you do what they're asking, you'll earn points; if you don't, you'll get a time-out"), her parents' warning would actually cause Amy to become more frustrated and agitated, her thinking increasingly disorganized and irrational, and her control over her words and actions greatly reduced. Amy's parents would interpret her increased intensity and failure to respond to their commands as an attempt to force them to "back down" or "give in" and would warn her of an impending time-out. Amy, now bereft of any semblance of rationality, would begin screaming and lashing out. Her parents would take Amy by the arm to escort her to time-out, an action that would further intensify her frustration and irrationality. Amy would resist being placed in time-out. Her parents would try to restrain her physically in time-out (many books no longer recommend this practice, but the book Amy's parents were using wasn't one of them) or confine her to her room until she calmed down. The struggle to keep Amy in time-out or confine her to her room would further intensify her explosion. She would try to hit, kick, bite, scratch, and spit on her parents. Once locked in her room—when her parents were actually able to get her there and keep her there—she would try to destroy anything she could get her hands on, including some of her favorite toys.

Eventually, meaning somewhere in the range of ten minutes to two hours, Amy would become completely exhausted and start to cry or fall asleep. Rationality would be restored. Her exhausted parents would be frustrated and angry and would hope that what they just did to their daughter—and endured themselves—was eventually going to pay off in the form of improved compliance. When Amy would finally emerge from her room, she would be remorseful. The parents would, in a firm tone, re-issue the direction that started the whole episode in the first place.

What's the matter with this picture? Was Amy's noncompliance truly planned, purposeful, and intentional? Are the terms oppositional, noncompliant, defiant, manipulative, coercive, attention seeking, unmotivated, and so forth, really the best ways to describe Amy? Are her parents truly lousy disciplinarians? Is a reward and punishment program really the best way to teach Amy how to be more flexible and to deal more adaptively with frustration?

No. No. No. No. And no again.

If a child has a reading disability, what's the appropriate intervention? Figure out why and teach the skills he lacks. If a child is delayed in the development of mathematics skills, what's the appropriate intervention? Figure out why and teach the skills he lacks. And if your child is challenged in the domains of flexibility and frustration tolerance, what should you do? Figure out why and teach the skills he lacks.

Unfortunately, we live in a society in which many adults, when faced with a child who isn't meeting expectations, can think of only one word: *Consequences*. That's a shame, because there are only two ways in which consequences are actually useful: (1) *to teach basic lessons about right from wrong* (such as don't hit, don't swear, don't explode); and (2) *to motivate people to behave appropriately*. But it's a very safe bet that your child already knows you don't want him to hit, swear, or explode, so it wouldn't make a great deal of sense to spend a lot of time using consequences to teach him something he already knows. And—this may be a little harder to believe—it's also a safe bet that your child is already motivated not to make himself and those around him miserable, so it wouldn't make a great deal of sense to spend a lot of time using consequences to give him the incentive to do well. *Children do well if they can.* If your child could do well, he would. He needs something else from you. Thankfully, there's a whole universe of options available to help your child besides consequences. Your journey into a new universe begins in the next chapter.

Question: Aren't flexibility and frustration tolerance critical skills? Doesn't my child have to change?

Answer: Flexibility and frustration tolerance are critical skills, and there may be some ways to teach your child how to be more flexible. But you may not be getting anywhere—or doing any productive teaching—by engaging in frequent battles with him whenever you try to force him to be more flexible.

Question: But if I don't teach my child how to be flexible, how will he learn?

Answer: If he's going to learn to be more flexible—and I'm optimistic that he can—it's not going to happen by your being a role model for inflexibility.

Question: But the old way worked for me; I'm just raising my kids the same way I was raised.

Answer: The way you were raised may have worked for you—and it seems to be working for your other children—but it's clearly not working as well for your explosive child.

Question: Don't I need to set a precedent now so my child knows who's boss and doesn't think he can always get his way?

Answer: Your explosive child already knows you're the boss and already knows he can't always get his way. Mission accomplished. So you can probably stop setting precedents and teaching him who's the boss and that he can't always get his way. He needs something else from you.

Question: I don't know what else to do.

Answer: You won't be able to say that after you're through reading this book.

6

Plan B

Old patterns are hard to break, so repetition is a crucial ingredient for keeping things moving in the right direction. Toward this end, here are some of the important points we want to keep fresh:

- Flexibility and tolerance for frustration are skills. Because your child lacks thinking skills (pathways), he has difficulty handling frustration responding to the world in an adaptable, flexible manner. Fortunately, these skills can be learned.

- Conventional explanations for your child's explosions—inept parenting, poor motivation, attention seeking, and the lack of appreciation for who's boss—may not be accurate, so conventional parenting practices and motivational programs flowing from these explanations may be mismatched to his needs. Your child may require a different approach.

- As you've probably already discovered, it's unlikely that the explosions you've been inducing and enduring have taught your child anything productive or led to any meaningful positive change in his behavior.

A FEW IMPORTANT THEMES

Before we get to the actual nuts and bolts of Collaborative Problem Solving (often referred to henceforth simply as CPS), let's take a few pages to discuss how to create an atmosphere that is more "user-friendly" for your explosive child, so as to set the stage for the hard work that lies ahead. First, *it's going to be important to make sure that all the adults who interact with your child have a clear understanding of his difficulties*. One child with whom I was working had been melting down far less frequently at home and school, and his parents and teachers and I had started thinking we were on Easy

Street—until his physical education teacher, whom we had neglected to enlighten, demanded that the child wear a sweatshirt outside on a fifty-five-degree day. After about three minutes of what might best be called reciprocal inflexibility, the child put his fist through a window. The point here is that getting everyone on the same wavelength is crucial. If that's not possible, then getting as many people as possible on the same wavelength is the goal. Better to have some people being responsive to your child's needs than none.

Second, *it may be necessary to put some of your parenting agenda on the back burner, at least temporarily*. Your child has proven beyond a doubt that he can't handle all the frustrations presently on his radar screen. If you clear the screen of some unnecessary frustrations and (perhaps unrealistic) goals, his global level of frustration should decrease and he should be able to more successfully work with you to deal with the frustrations and goals that remain. If your child is exploding less often, the general level of tension and hostility in your family should diminish as well. While many parents and teachers can appreciate the wisdom of reducing the overall demands for flexibility and frustration tolerance being placed on a child, they often need help understanding how to do it. They also want reassurance that the child will not come to view them as pushovers. Here's your reassurance: *There is absolutely nothing about Collaborative*

Problem Solving that will have you feeling like a pushover.

Third, if you haven't already, *you may have to come to grips with the fact that your child is a little different.* Yours is not a "business as usual" child. So if you were hoping for the standard, easygoing child, it's not in the cards. Luckily, the definition of good parenting (and good teaching) is *"being responsive to the hand you've been dealt."* Chapter 3 provided you with a better sense of the hand you've been dealt. The rest of this book is about how to be more responsive to that hand.

Fourth—and this was mentioned in passing earlier but is about to become very important—*explosions are actually highly predictable*. Not all explosions are predictable, but most are. And if they're predictable, you can solve the problems that cause them proactively—in advance. In each child and family, there are usually somewhere between five and ten triggers that contribute to explosions on a weekly basis. In Chapter 3 these were referred to as problems that have yet to be solved. Once these problems are durably solved, they won't cause explosions anymore.

So here's your first homework assignment: *For the next week, keep a record of the problems that caused your child to become frustrated.* This is your list of problems to be solved; it may include things like waking up and getting out of bed in the morning, getting ready for school, sensory hypersensitivities, doing homework, getting ready for bed at night, boredom, shifting from one activity to another, sibling interactions, being hungry just before dinner, food choices or quantities, clothing choices, being surprised by a sudden change in plans, taking medicine. But those are just some of the possibilities. Get your list ready. We've got problems to solve!

THREE OPTIONS

There are basically three ways to handle a problem or unmet expectation with a child. We used to call these options the three "baskets." (This term came from the early days of the CPS approach, when we felt that people might benefit from the visual metaphor of having three baskets in front of them and depositing different problems or unmet expectations into the baskets depending on how each was to be handled.) Now we call them Plans, as in Plan A, Plan B, and Plan C. It's important to emphasize that the Plans come into play only when there is a problem or unmet expectation. If your child is meeting an expectation, then you don't need a Plan. For example, if your child is completing his homework to your satisfaction and without exploding, you don't need a Plan because your expectation is being met. If your child is brushing his teeth to your satisfaction and without exploding, you don't need a Plan because the expectation is being met. But if your child is *not* meeting your homework completion or teeth brushing expectations or if these expectations heighten the likelihood of explosions, you need a Plan.

Many people think the terminology "Plan A" refers to the *preferred* plan. Not in this book. In this book Plan A refers to handling a problem or unmet expectation through the *imposition of adult will*. Plan C involves *dropping the expectation completely,* at least for now. And Plan B involves doing the name of the approach—*Collaborative Problem Solving*—and engaging the child in a discussion in which *the problem or unmet expectation is resolved in a mutually satisfactory manner*. If you intend to follow the advice in this book, the Plans are your future. One of them in particular. Let's take a closer look.

PLAN A

If your child isn't meeting a given expectation and you respond by imposing your will—i.e., by saying things like "No," "You must," or "You can't"—you're using Plan A. So if your child says, "I'm too tired to do my homework tonight," a potential Plan A response would be, "But you must." If your child says, "I want to take a break from brushing my teeth tonight," a potential Plan A response would be, "No." Of course, "I'm not interested in discussing it," "I didn't say you had a choice," "Get your butt in gear," and the threat or imposition of consequences are Plan A responses as well.

Now, these might sound like perfectly ordinary, reasonable responses, but only if you have a perfectly ordinary, reasonable child. You don't. In the case of explosive kids, Plan A—imposing your will—*greatly heightens the likelihood of an explosion*. Why? Because you're throwing Plan A at a kid who doesn't have a Plan A brain. Let's go back to the description of an explosive outburst you read in Chapter 2:

An explosive outburst—like other forms of maladaptive behavior—occurs when the cognitive demands being placed upon a person outstrip that person's capacity to respond adaptively.

If you throw Plan A at a kid who doesn't have a Plan A brain, you've placed a cognitive demand upon him that outstrips his capacity to respond adaptively. *Kaboom*. Indeed, when we "rewind the tape" on the vast majority of explosions in children, what do we find? An adult using Plan A.

Why doesn't your child have a Plan A brain? Pathways.

Is Plan A going to be an integral part of helping your child overcome his learning disability in the domains of flexibility and frustration tolerance? No, it's not.

Can you maintain your status as an authority figure,

pursue your expectations, and live happily with your child without Plan A? Yes, you most certainly can.

PLAN C

As you read above, Plan C involves dropping a given expectation completely, at least temporarily. You know you're using Plan C if you say either nothing at all or OK in response to a problem or unmet expectation. So if your child says, "I'm too tired to do my homework tonight," a Plan C response would be, "OK." If you've noticed that your child is getting into bed without brushing his teeth, a Plan C response would be to say nothing at all.

There's an up side to Plan C: It helps you prevent an explosion. But there's also a down side: You've dropped your expectation completely, at least for now. Of course, as discussed earlier in this chapter, dropping some of your expectations completely can also be a very good thing, especially in the case of extremely volatile and unstable explosive kids, for it can help such kids be more available to discuss the frustrations that remain. Some people rely exclusively on medicine to reduce a child's volatility and instability, and for some children medicine can be indispensable. But many kids can be stabilized and helped to be more available without medicine by temporarily reducing expectations through use of Plan C.

At first glance, many people come to the quick conclusion that Plan C is the equivalent of giving in. Actually, giving in is what happens when you start off using Plan A and end up using Plan C because your child made your life miserable. When you intentionally use Plan C, you are proactively deciding to drop a given expectation, either because you've decided it was unrealistic in the first place or because you've got bigger fish to fry.

For example, one child was remarkably particular about what foods he was willing to eat: certain cereals for breakfast and pizza for dinner. His parents were quite determined—as evidenced by their relentless badgering and nagging (badgering and nagging, by the way, are half-hearted forms of Plan A)—that he have a balanced diet but weren't able to shove lima beans down their son's throat. This example of reciprocal inflexibility led to at least two explosions a day (at breakfast and dinner). Except in extreme cases, such as bona fide eating disorders, issues associated with diabetes, and so forth, a Plan C approach to food is probably indicated with these picky-eating explosive children. In other words, they won't starve. And, indeed, this child wasn't starving. "Eating a variety of foods" was handled with Plan C, explosions over this issue were eliminated, other more pressing issues were addressed, and the food trigger was eventually addressed without aid of Plan A. The child is now eating a somewhat wider variety of foods, and he actually goes to the supermarket with his mother to make his own selections.

Another child, Eduardo, routinely exploded whenever

his mother brought him to the supermarket. Eduardo exploded in other situations as well, of course, but none as predictably as the supermarket. Maybe it was the overstimulation, maybe it was the fact that he had very inflexible ideas about the foods he wanted his mother to buy (most of which were not at the top of his mother's list). Whatever the reason, no matter what the mother tried—preparing him in advance for trips, rewarding him for good behavior and punishing him for inappropriate behavior, making shorter trips, having Grandma accompany them, trying to steer him around the aisles where meltdowns seemed to occur most often, agreeing that he could select one or two of the foods on his list—he still routinely exploded when she brought him to the supermarket. The mother finally came to the conclusion that mastery of the demands of the supermarket—staying next to the shopping cart, not demanding the purchase of every high-sugar cereal on the shelves, being patient in the checkout line—simply wasn't going to improve at that point in her son's development. She decided he'd be much better off if she eliminated the expectation that her son accompany her to the supermarket (Plan C).

Mother: But he can't avoid supermarkets forever, right?

Therapist: Right. Luckily, going to the supermarket is not critical to Eduardo's existence right now.

Mother: When should I try taking him into supermarkets again?

Therapist: When you've resolved some of the more important triggers on your list, and when you think he can do it.

Therapist: It's not always easy for my mother to watch him for me.

Me: I know. But it's even harder—and a lot more detrimental to your relationship with your son—to have him exploding every time you take him to the supermarket.

"Business as usual" is a fine idea, but only if you have a "business as usual" kid. You don't.

What other triggers might warrant a Plan C response, at least temporarily? That varies from family to family, and depends a lot on the child's level of instability. But triggers that have made it into Plan C for some kids have included brushing teeth, food choices, exercising, doing homework, using good table manners, getting to school on time, and even swearing. Naturally, all of these triggers eventually were handled using Plan B once the child had stabilized and other more pressing problems had been solved.

Let's turn now to the most important option, the one upon which the success of the CPS model hinges.

PLAN B

As you've read, Plan B involves doing the name of the approach: Collaborative Problem Solving. What's the main activity of Plan B? Discuss and work out mutually satisfactory solutions to the problems that have been causing your child (and perhaps you, too) to behave maladaptively.

Now, according to many popular parenting books, you should never work things out with a child. According to the book you're reading right now, working things out with your child can be an extremely effective way to pursue your expectations, while simultaneously reducing the likelihood of an explosion, while simultaneously helping your child learn skills he clearly lacks. You don't lose any authority when using Plan B. None.

Your role when using Plan B is that of *surrogate frontal lobe.* That is, you're going to be doing the thinking for your child that he's currently incapable of doing on his own; you're going to serve as his tour guide through frustration. Here's what a lot of folks think when they first contemplate being a surrogate frontal lobe: Wait a second, my kid's going to need a surrogate frontal lobe for the rest of his life? Actually, the reason you're being a surrogate frontal lobe now is so that your child won't need a surrogate frontal lobe for the rest of his life. Once you've taught your child the skills he needs to successfully navigate frustrations and demands for flexibility on his own, you're fired. Who fired you? He did. Why'd he fire you? Because *children do well if they can*. Same as with any other learning disability.

This next part is important. There are two ways to do Plan B: *Emergency Plan B* and *Proactive Plan B*. On first hearing about Plan B, many folks come to the erroneous conclusion that the best time to use Plan B is just as a child is becoming frustrated. That's Emergency Plan B, and it's actually not the best timing because the child is already getting heated up. Few of us do our clearest thinking when we're heated up. As discussed earlier, most explosions are highly predictable. Thus, there's no reason to wait until the child gets heated up yet again to try to solve the problem that's been causing explosions for a very long time. The goal is to get the problem solved proactively—before it comes up again. That's Proactive Plan B.

For example, if your child always balks at brushing his teeth, the best time to have a Plan B discussion with him is before he's faced with the task of teeth brushing again rather than in the heat of the moment. If your child routinely has difficulty with his homework, the time to have a Plan B discussion aimed at solving that problem is before he's struggling with his homework the next time.

This next part is absolutely crucial. There are three steps for doing Plan B:

1. *Empathy (plus Reassurance)*
2. *Define the problem*
3. *Invitation*

If you do the above three steps in the prescribed order, you're doing Plan B. If you don't do the above three steps in the prescribed order, you're not doing Plan B. So we'd better take a closer look at these three steps.

Empathy

Empathy is the first step of Plan B for a few reasons. First, empathy keeps people calm, so it's a good way to help your child stay rational enough to actually converse with you. If you don't keep him calm, then the problem causing him frustration won't get solved because the conversation won't take place.

Empathy also ensures that your child's concern is on the table. Just like adults, kids have legitimate concerns: hunger, fatigue, fears, a desire to buy or do certain things, a desire to be less hot or less cold, and so forth. Sadly, most kids are accustomed to having their concerns blown off the table by adults who have concerns of their own.

It's not exactly clear why you'd want to blow any child's concern off the table, but it should be crystal clear why you wouldn't want to do it with an explosive child. You don't lose any authority by empathizing. But you do keep him calm and enter his concern into consideration.

How do you empathize? Basically, by repeating the child's concern back to him, sticking closely to his exact words. Some call this reflective listening. Let's practice.

Child: The medicine is making me sick to my stomach.
Adult (Empathy): The medicine is making you sick to your stomach.

Child: I'm worried that the movie will be too scary.
Adult (Empathy): You're worried that the movie will be too scary.

Child: I'm too tired to do my homework.
Adult (Empathy): You're too tired to do your homework.

Sounds pretty straightforward, yes? Actually, it turns out that, for a lot of adults, empathizing isn't nearly as easy as it seems. And empathy is made more difficult by the fact that children are seldom highly specific about their concerns. In fact, children (like adults) are more likely to put a solution on the table than a concern. Your job? Make sure it's the child's concern that ultimately makes it onto the table. If you don't know what the child's concern is, you'll need to find out, generally by asking, "What's up?" If he doesn't know what his concern is, you'll have to take educated guesses (as discussed in detail in Chapter 8). Let's practice again.

Child: I'm not taking my meds. (This isn't a concern; it's a solution to a concern.)

Adult (Initial Empathy): You're not taking your meds. What's up?

Child: It's making me sick to my stomach. (Ah, now we have a concern to put on the table, and a good one at that.)

Adult (Refined Empathy): It's making you sick to your stomach.

Child: I'm not going with you to the movies. (Again, a solution, not a concern.)

Adult (Initial Empathy): You're not going with us to the movies. What's up?

Child: It might be too scary for me. (We wouldn't want to blow that concern off the table.)

Adult (Refined Empathy): You're worried that the movie might be too scary for you.

Child: I'm not doing my homework.
Adult (Initial Empathy): You're not doing your homework. What's up?
Child: It's too hard for me.
Adult (Refined Empathy): It's too hard for you.

Along these lines, it's a good idea to use low-risk empathy rather than jump to conclusions about what the child is trying to say. For example, if a child says, "I want pizza," low-risk empathy and clarifying would be, "You want pizza. What's up?" But a lot of people might respond to "I want pizza" with "You must be hungry." While the odds are pretty good that you're correct in making that assumption, there exists the possibility that you're wrong. For example, the child may not be hungry; he may, for example, be a black-and-white thinker who was promised pizza earlier in the day. Why would this be a problem? Because he may not have the wherewithal to correct you, in which case your well-intentioned stab at empathy could actually precipitate an explosion. Low-risk empathy is typically a safer bet.

By the way, after about a week of reflective listening, adolescents in particular are likely to ask, "Why are you saying everything I just said?" or "You sound like a psychologist." If an adolescent (or child) objects to the reflective listening form of empathy, a simple "I hear ya" will usually suffice instead.

Sometimes empathy alone isn't completely sufficient for keeping the child calm. He might need some reassurance as well. Reassurance about what? Reassurance that you're not using Plan A. You see, it's a pretty safe bet he's had a lot more Plan A in his life than Plan B, so he's probably still betting on the Plan A horse. Which means that, early in your attempts to use Plan A, he may still get heated up because he's not yet accustomed to your trying to collaborate with him to solve problems. So he's going to need some reassurance on that count. But since he doesn't know what Plan A is, you can't say, "I'm not using Plan A." Instead, you should say something like, "I'm not saying you have to" or "I'm not saying no." Of course, you're not saying "yes," either. Empathy is neither "yes" nor "no." It's neither agreeing nor disagreeing. It simply keeps the child (and you) calm and gets his concern on the table. So here's the whole empathy step, from start to finish:

Child: I want pizza.
Adult (Initial Empathy): You want pizza. What's up?
Child: I'm hungry.
Adult (Refined Empathy, plus Reassurance): You're hungry. I'm not saying you can't have pizza.

One last point, before we move on to the next step. All of the dialogues above are actually examples of *Emergency* Plan B. But since explosions are highly predictable, it's likely that the child's concerns over taking his medicine have come up before, that this isn't the first time homework has been an issue, and that scary movies have been a concern for your child previously. Here's how the empathy step would sound if we were attempting Proactive Plan B:

Adult (Empathy, using Proactive B): I know that your medicine has been making you sick to your stomach and that you're not too happy about that.

Adult (Empathy, using Proactive B): We were thinking of going to the movies this afternoon and I know that sometimes you don't want to go because you're worried there will be scary parts.

Adult (Empathy, using Proactive B, with an attempt to clarify): I've noticed that homework has been a struggle lately. But I don't think I understand why that is. What's up with the homework?

Child: It's too hard for me.

Adult (Refined Empathy, with another attempt to clarify): It's too hard for you. Is there a certain part that's hard for you?

Child: The writing part. At school they don't make me do as much writing as you do.

Adult (Refined Empathy): Ah, the writing part is hard for you and I make you do more writing than they do at school.

Define the Problem

It is in the second step of Plan B that the adult places his or her concern on the table. We call this the Define the Problem step because we define a problem simply as *two concerns that have yet to be reconciled*: your child's and yours. Plan B is the only approach to problems or unmet expectations where there are two concerns on the table. If the only concern on the table is the Adult's concern, you're using Plan A. If the only concern on the table is the Child's, you're using Plan C. If both concerns are on the table, you're using Plan B.

Now, adults are just as prone to putting solutions (instead of concerns) on the table as children are. Plan B is dead in the water if there are two solutions on the table. Indeed, an adult putting a solution on the table usually signals that the discussion has shifted from Plan B to Plan A. Examples: "You have to go to the movies because I can't send your brother to the theater alone;" "You don't want to do your homework? Just do it and get it over with!" and "If you don't take your meds I'm not taking you to soccer practice."

Why are adults so inclined to put solutions on the table instead of concerns? Because they were well trained by their predecessors! So this can take a little practice. Here are some examples of how it should sound (note that all are continuations of the *Proactive* Plan B discussions above):

Adult (Empathy): I know that your medicine has been making you sick to your stomach and that you're not too happy about that.

Child: Yeah.

Adult (Define the Problem): I'm not too happy about it either. The thing is, I'm a little worried about what will happen if we just yank you off the meds without talking to Dr. Lazarus. Plus, the medicine seems to be helping you control your temper a little better.

Adult (Empathy): We were thinking of going to the movies this afternoon and I know that sometimes you don't want to go because you're worried that there will be scary parts.

Child: I don't like scary movies.

Adult (Reassurance and Define the Problem): I know, and I'm not saying you have to go to a scary movie. The thing is, your brother is really looking forward to going to the movies and I can't send him to the movies alone.

Adult (Empathy, with an attempt to clarify): I've noticed that homework has been a struggle lately. But I don't think I understand why that is. What's up with the homework?

Child: It's too hard for me.

Adult (Refined Empathy, with another attempt to clarify): It's too hard for you. Is there a certain part that's hard for you?

Child: The writing part. At school they don't make me do as much writing as you do.

Adult (Refined Empathy): Ah, the writing part is hard for you and I make you do more writing than they do at school.

Child: Yeah.

Adult (Define the Problem): I didn't know they don't make you write as much at school. I guess I'm just concerned that if you don't practice the writing, then it will always be really hard for you.

You've got two concerns on the table. No turning back now.

Invitation

The third step of Plan B entails having the child and adult brainstorm potential solutions to the problem that has now been defined by their respective concerns. This step is called the invitation because the adult is actually *inviting* the child to solve the problem collaboratively by saying something like, "Let's think about how we can solve this problem" or "Let's think about how we can work that out." The Invitation lets the child know that solving the problem is something you're doing *with* him—in other words, together—rather than *to* him.

After the child has been invited to solve the problem collaboratively, he is then given first crack at generating a solution ("Do you have any ideas?"). *This doesn't mean the burden for solving the problem has been placed upon the child.* But it is good strategy, especially for children who are accustomed to having parental will imposed upon them. The burden for solving the problem is placed upon the Problem Solving Team: your child and you.

Many parents, in their eagerness to solve the problem, forget the Invitation. This means that, just as they are at the precipice of actually collaborating with their child, they impose their will. You see, somewhere between childhood and adulthood, many people arrived at the conclusion that the only person capable of coming up with a good solution to a problem is the adult. Where does that very unfortunate notion come from? Predecessors. While there is some chance that your child won't be able to think of any solutions (an issue discussed in greater detail in Chapter 8), there's actually an outstanding chance your child *can* think of good solutions—ones that will take your combined concerns into account—

and has been waiting (not so patiently) for you to give him the chance. So, as it relates to solving problems with your child, here's an important theme: *Don't be a genius.*

You'd think that most adults would breathe a sigh of relief at the news that they no longer need to come up with an immediate, ingenious solution to a problem. In truth, it takes some folks some getting used to. Most difficult problems don't get solved in a nanosecond. Most difficult problems that get solved in a nanosecond aren't durably solved anyway. Solving a difficult problem *durably* requires reflection, consideration, time, and a willingness to let the process of exploring solutions unfold without premature interruption. If you're thinking that Plan B discussions can sometimes take a long time, you're right. But explosions take much longer.

A few more important themes before we practice. Many adults begin Plan B discussions with very strong notions about how a problem will be solved. It's not terrible to have some ideas about how a problem can be solved, so long as you remember that Plan B is not "tricky" Plan A. When you use Plan B, you do so with the understanding that the solution is not predetermined. One father who had failed to remember this once said, "I don't use Plan B unless I already know how the problem is going to be solved." If you already know how the problem is going to be solved before the discussion takes place, then you're not using Plan B—you're using Plan A.

What's the definition of an ingenious solution? *Any*

solution that is doable (by both parties), realistic, and mutually satisfactory. If a solution isn't doable, realistic, and mutually satisfactory, the problem isn't solved yet and the Problem Solving Team is still working on it.

Some kids' first stab at a solution is to simply repeat what they wanted in the first place (for example, "I'm not going to the movies"). This is usually a sign that the child is not yet very good at generating solutions that are mutually satisfactory. But if you want him to be *thinking* rather than exploding about problems, the last thing you'd want to do is tell him he's come up with a bad idea. Instead, simply remind him that the goal is to come up with a solution that works for both of you, perhaps by saying, "Well, that's an idea. But that solution would make you happy—because then you wouldn't have to worry about being scared—but it probably wouldn't make your brother happy, since he really wants to go to the movies. Let's see if we can come up with an idea that will make us all happy." In other words, there's no such thing as a bad solution—only solutions that aren't realistic, doable, or mutually satisfactory.

By the way, the *mutually satisfactory* part should be of great comfort to adults who feared that, in using Plan B, their concerns would not be addressed. If a solution is mutually satisfactory, then by definition your concerns have been addressed. So if you were thinking that Plan A is the only mechanism by which adults can set limits, you were mistaken. The definition of limit setting is *en-*

suring that your concerns are addressed. Thus, you're setting limits when using Plan B as well. Of course, the mutually satisfactory part also has a calming effect on explosive children, who had become accustomed to exploding when their concerns were blown off the table by adults using Plan A. If your concerns are being addressed with Plan B—without causing your child to explode—then why do you still need Plan A? Maybe you don't.

The *doable* and *realistic* parts are important, too. Plan B isn't an exercise in wishful thinking. If you can't do the solution that's being agreed to, then don't agree to it just to end the conversation. That's called "explosion deferred" but not "problem solved." Likewise, if you don't think your child can do the solution that's being agreed to, then don't agree to it just to end the conversation. You're the surrogate frontal lobe—make sure he takes a moment to consider whether he can actually do what he's agreeing to do. ("You sure you can do that? Let's make sure we come up with a solution we can both do.")

Let's see how the three steps would look all together (using Proactive Plan B), assuming that things are going really smoothly (we'll get to problems people encounter in using Plan B soon enough):

Adult (Empathy): I know that your medicine has been making you sick to your stomach and that you're not too happy about that.

Child: Yeah.

Adult (Define the Problem, then Invitation): I'm not too happy about it either. The thing is, I'm a little worried about what will happen if we just yank you off the meds without talking to Dr. Lazarus. Plus, the medicine seems to be helping you control your temper a little better. Let's think about what we can do about that . . . do you have any ideas?

Child: I don't want to take my medicine.

Adult: I know. I'm very sorry it's making you sick to your stomach. I just don't want to make you sicker by having you stop taking it before Dr. Lazarus says it's OK.

Child: Can you call him?

Adult: I tried. He hasn't called back yet. I guess I could page him.

Child: Yes, page him!

Adult: I think that's probably the best idea. We have an appointment with him next week. You don't think you could take the medicine until the appointment and then we'll ask him what we should do?

Child: It's making me sick to my stomach!

Adult: OK, I'll page him and he can tell us what to do. I don't think he's going to say you can stop taking it completely, though, so we need to be ready if he says you should keep taking it. Maybe he's had other kids who got sick to their stomach on this medicine and he'll know what worked for them.

Adult (Empathy): We were thinking of going to the movies this afternoon, and I know that sometimes you don't want to go because you're worried there will be scary parts.

Child: I don't like scary movies.

Adult (Define the Problem, Reassurance, Invitation): I know, and I'm not saying you have to go to a scary movie. The thing is, your brother is really looking forward to going to the movies and I can't send him to the movies alone. Let's think of how we could work this out. Do you have any ideas?

Child: We could not go to the movies.

Adult: There's an idea. The thing is, if we don't go to the movies, you'd be very happy, but your brother would be very unhappy. Let's see if we can come up with an idea that would make us all happy.

Child: We could go to a movie that's not scary.

Adult: We could. How about we go get the movie section from the newspaper and see if there are any movies out that aren't scary that you and your brother would both want to see. If we can find one, then we could still go to the movies, but you wouldn't have to worry that it's too scary. Yes?

Adult (Empathy, with an attempt to clarify): I've noticed that homework has been a struggle for us lately. But I don't think I understand why that is. What's up with the homework?

Child: It's too hard for me.

Adult (Refined Empathy, with another attempt to clarify): It's too hard for you. Is there a certain part that's hard for you?

Child: The writing part. At school they don't make me do as much writing as you do.

Adult (Refined Empathy): Ah, the writing part is hard for you and I make you do more writing at home than they do at school.

Child: Yeah.

Adult (Define the Problem): I didn't know they don't make you write as much at school. I guess I'm just concerned that if you don't practice the writing, then it will always be really hard for you.

Child: I do practice the writing at school. But the homework isn't supposed to be to practice writing—it's supposed to be to practice spelling!

Adult (Reassurance, plus Invitation): I'm not saying you have to do the writing at home. I just want to make sure you're getting as much writing practice as you need. Let's think of what we can do about this problem. What do you think?

Child: I get plenty of writing practice at school!

Adult: Yes, so you said. I think the problem here is

that I thought I was supposed to be practicing writing with you at home, too. But I haven't spoken to Mrs. Andrews lately, so, to tell you the truth, I'm not exactly clear about what I'm supposed to be doing at home.

Child: Why don't you talk to Mrs. Andrews and ask her!

Adult: I'm starting to think that's a very good idea. Then you wouldn't have to do writing you're not supposed to be doing—if that's what she says—and I'd know you were getting enough writing practice. Does that solution work for you?

Child: Yes.

Adult: It works for me, too. Thanks for talking about this with me, pal.

It's true, Plan B isn't usually this easy, especially early on. For example, sometimes kids (and even adults) get pretty heated up with Plan B. As noted above, sometimes this is because history has taught them that disagreements are always handled using Plan A. It may take a while (and a lot of Plan B) for the child's instantaneous heated reaction to disagreements to subside. But let's take a look at what things might look like when there's added heat early in the Plan B process (and when a predictable problem that has yet to be solved is handled emergently rather than proactively). Notice that the steps are the same, but there's just added heat. Stay the course.

Mother: Davis, it's time to go to your swim lesson.

Davis (playing with Legos at the kitchen table): I'm not going. I hate swim lessons.

Mother (now using Emergency Plan B): Davis, we have a problem, because your brother has a swim lesson, too, and I can't leave you home alone.

Davis: I don't care! I'm not going!

Mother: We need to find a way to work this out. You don't want to go to your swim lesson, but I need to take—

Davis (slamming his fist on the table, red-faced): HOW MANY TIMES DO I HAVE TO TELL YOU?! I HATE SWIMMING! I'M NOT GOING! GET AWAY FROM ME!

Mother: Davis, I didn't say you had to go to your swim lesson. I said we have to find a way to work this out. That's different.

Davis: I'm sick of working things out. IF YOU DON'T SHUT UP, I'M GOING TO KILL YOU!

Davis's brother: Mom, I'm gonna be late for my swim lesson!

Mother, to brother: Alden, can you go get my purse? I think it's in my bedroom.

Mother, to Davis (Reassurance, plus Invitation): Davis, I'm not saying you have to go to your swim lesson. I'm just trying to think of how we can get your brother to his swim lesson without me leaving you home alone. Do you have any ideas?

Davis: No!

Mother: I might have an idea. Would you like to hear it?

Davis: Fine!

Mother: Can you take the Legos with you and you can work on your Legos while your brother is at his swim lesson?

Davis: The pieces will break apart. I don't want to go.

Mother: I understand that you don't want to go. I'm not saying you have to take your swim lesson. But I can't leave you home alone. The only way I can think of to work this out is for you to come with me and bring the Legos along. If you have a different idea, I'm happy to listen.

Davis: [no response]

Mother: What do you think?

Alden (back from retrieving the purse): I'm going to be late!

Davis, to his brother: SHUT UP, JERK!

Alden: No, you shut up!

Mother, to Alden: Alden, I want you to go wait for me by the front door. Now!

Alden: He told me to shut up!

Mother: I heard what he told you. It wasn't very nice. Now go wait for me by the front door.

Mother, to Davis: Davis, the only way I can think of to work this out is for you to bring the Legos with you while your brother is at his swim lesson. If you can think of other solutions, I'm happy to listen.

Davis (starting to pack up his Legos): I'm not taking a swim lesson, so don't try to make me. Look! I told you the Legos were going to break apart!

Mother (switching to the new problem): Let's think of how we can transport the Legos so they don't fall apart. Thanks for trying to work this out.

Davis: I wasn't trying to work it out.

Mother: Well, you did a good job anyway.

Is the swimming lesson problem solved durably? Not yet. That problem should be the topic of a Proactive Plan B discussion within the next few days so it gets solved once and for all.

There's much more to cover about Plan B, but you've been given a lot to digest already. And upon first reading about the Plans, many adults come to some instantaneous misconceptions. So let's get a few things cleared up before they cause trouble.

Many people have the misconception that the CPS model requires that they suspend all of their expectations in order to reduce their child's explosions. It sounds something like this: "So let me get this straight, I'm supposed to drop all my expectations so my kid doesn't explode anymore?" Wrong. Dead wrong. Expectations are a good thing, especially the realistic variety. The CPS model does require that adults (1) consider whether, given the hand they've been dealt, their expectations for their child are truly realistic; (2) think about whether some expectations need to be eliminated (at least for the time being) to set the stage for the child to be more "available" to discuss and resolve more pressing problems; and (3) begin responding to unmet expectations using Plan B, given that Plan A hasn't exactly gotten the job done.

Many people also believe that the Plans are a ranking system for expectations. Here's how that sounds: "So the stuff I really carc about, that's Plan A. And the stuff I sort of care about, that's Plan B. And the stuff I don't care about at all, that's Plan C. Yes?" No. *The Plans are not a ranking system*. Each Plan represents a distinct way of responding to unmet expectations. With Plan A, you're imposing your will and greatly heightening the likelihood of explosions. With Plan C, you're dropping the expectation completely, at least temporarily. And with Plan B, you're discussing and working out solutions that are realistic, doable, and mutually satisfactory.

Some folks have the misconception that Plan B is the *average* of Plans A and C. Not so. Prior to learning about Plan B, many parents thought they had only two options: impose their will (Plan A) or drop their expectations (Plan C). *If you're using only Plans A and C, then all you're really doing is picking your battles.* But the combination of those two options brings you no closer to collaboratively and durably solving problems with your child.

Finally, some people think Plan B is supposed to work like magic. Plan B isn't magic. It's the hard work of two people (you and your child) putting their respective concerns on the table and putting their heads together to solve a problem that has been causing explosions and ill will for a very long time. Some problems require more than one conversation. Sometimes things get hot enough with Plan B to necessitate that the participants take a break from the action ("I think we're starting to get upset at each other, and that wasn't the goal of having this discussion. Maybe we should stop talking for a while and come back to it later"). And sometimes the first Plan B solution doesn't get the job done. That's not the signal to abandon ship. That's just a sign that the solution you both thought would accomplish the mission didn't accomplish the mission (a fairly common scenario in the human experience!). Most durable solutions are the byproduct of previous solutions that didn't quite get the job done.

Now, in the beginning of this chapter you were assigned the task of making a list of the problems that are routinely causing your child to become frustrated. This is your list of "problems that have yet to be solved." Now comes your next assignment. *Pick one or two of these prob-*

lems and try using Proactive Plan B with your child at an opportune time. If it goes well, terrific. If it doesn't go well, pay special attention to Chapters 7 and 8.

Need a brief summary of what you've just read? Here goes:

- There are three options for responding to problems or unmet expectations: impose your will (Plan A); drop the expectation completely, at least for now (Plan C); and work out a solution that is realistic, doable, and mutually satisfactory (Plan B).
    - With Plan A, you're pursuing your expectation but greatly heightening the likelihood of an explosion.
    - With Plan C, you're eliminating the potential for an explosion but not pursuing your expectation.
    - With Plan B, you're reducing the likelihood of an explosion and pursuing your expectation.

- Any unmet expectation that can be responded to by using Plan A can also be responded to by using Plan B. In other words, you're setting limits with Plan A, and you're setting limits with Plan B, but in very different ways. You don't lose any authority using Plan B. None.

- Plan B consists of three steps: Empathy (plus Reassurance), Define the Problem, and the Invitation. If you don't do the three steps in order, you're not doing Plan B. If there aren't two concerns on the table, you're not doing Plan B. And make sure there are two concerns on the table instead of two solutions, or the problem won't get solved.

- There are two forms of Plan B: Emergency B and Proactive B. Calm, rational discussions are usually tougher with Emergency B because of added heat; Proactive B is more likely to lead to durable solutions.

- Skillful execution of Plan B is hard, and it takes time to get good at it. The more you practice, the easier Plan B becomes. Plan B isn't something you do two or three times before returning to your old way of doing things. It's not a technique; it's a way of life.

- There are lots of things that can interfere with successful execution of Plan B. So don't get discouraged if things don't go swimmingly in the beginning. You don't fix a reading disability in a week. You don't fix this learning disability—or the habit of responding to your child with Plan A—in a week, either.

Let's finish this chapter with a few more examples of Emergency Plan B before moving to a more advanced discussion of Plan B and more examples of Proactive Plan B.

DRAMA IN REAL LIFE

Mickey, Minnie . . . Meltdown?

Remember Casey from Chapter 4? He and his parents and sister took a trip to Walt Disney World, and their first day went wonderfully. They were a pretty tired*, hungry* crew as they left* the Magic Kingdom on their way back to their hotel. (The asterisks designate well-known triggers: fatigue, hunger, and transitions.) Of course, this scenario had graver implications for Casey than for his sister. Just after they'd gotten outside the gates, Casey uttered the following, ominous request: "I want cotton candy."

"You can't have cotton candy because we're not going back into the park to look for it," said the father instinctively.

Casey stopped dead in his tracks. "I want cotton candy!" he said loudly.

The parents exchanged glances. They'd become pretty good at making quick decisions about what Plan they wanted to use and contemplated their three options. Plan A would only cause a lengthy explosion.

Nothing to be gained there. That left only Emergency Plan B and Plan C. Going back into the park for cotton candy would have been extremely inconvenient, and they wanted Casey to eat a good dinner. So Plan C wasn't ideal because they did have a concern to put on the table.

"Casey, I think you're very tired," the mother said, abandoning low-risk empathy.

"I want cotton candy!" he said, moving closer to the edge of the cliff.

The father jumped in with low-risk empathy and an attempt to clarify Casey's concern. "You want cotton candy!" he said. "What's up?"

"I want cotton candy!" said Casey. Maybe there was nothing to clarify.

"I think we need to find a way to work this out, Casey," the father said calmly. "You want cotton candy, and we want to get back to the hotel to get something to eat. Can you think of a good solution?"

"No!" Casey pouted, crossing his arms, still on the edge.

"Well, let's think about this for a second," said the father, crouching down next to his son. "We could look for someone selling cotton candy on the way back to the hotel . . . or we could just wait until we're back in the park tomorrow to buy cotton candy . . . or we could buy you something to snack on besides cotton candy. Can you think of something else you'd like to eat on the way home besides cotton candy?"

"I want cotton candy," whined Casey, but his tone suggested that rational thought might slowly be returning.

"Well, I'm not saying you can't have cotton candy, but I don't want to go back into the park. We could look for someone selling cotton candy on the way home," said the father. "Would that work for you?"

Casey started walking toward the car again.

"Can I have cotton candy, too?" asked Casey's sister.

The mother bit her lip. "Whatever we get, you can have some, too," she said.

Once in the car, the family spent the next ten minutes with their faces glued to the windows, scanning the horizon for potential cotton candy vendors. Casey's capacity for rational thought slowly returned. There was one small problem, of course: They hadn't yet come upon any stores that might be selling cotton candy. With Casey's capacity for rational thought somewhat restored, the father felt Casey might be able to handle the bad news without falling apart.

"I don't see anyone selling cotton candy, guys," he said. "But there's a McDonald's up ahead—should we see what kinds of snacks we can find there? Maybe some French fries?"

"Oh, boy, McDonald's!" exclaimed Casey.

"Don't forget, this is just a snack, guys," said the mother.

Casey rushed into the McDonald's, ate his fries, and wound up eating a decent dinner back at the hotel.

Had the parents decided to handle the cotton candy problem with Plan A, they would likely have endured yet another long explosion. Had they decided to handle things using Plan C, they would have gone back into the park for cotton candy. By deciding to use Plan B, they averted an explosion on an important issue. Their son still ate some of what they wanted him to eat, and they gave themselves, Casey, and his sister some additional practice at solving problems collaboratively. They were being responsive to the hand they'd been dealt and were still, without doubt, authority figures.

DRAMA IN REAL LIFE

Is This Starting to Register?

Remember Helen, the girl who wanted macaroni and cheese instead of chili in chapter 4? One night, Helen had somehow decided that she wanted to do her homework sitting atop the "register" in the kitchen. Helen's father objected to her doing her homework sitting atop the register. This minor disagreement—which had never arisen before—had the potential to totally disrupt Helen's completion of her homework by inducing a prolonged explosion.

"Helen, I don't want you to do your homework sitting on the register," said the father.

"I want to," Helen whined.

"Helen, I want you to come over to the kitchen table and do your homework," commanded the father, now using Plan A.

"I want to sit here!" Helen whined with a little more fervor.

The father caught himself. Continue with Plan A, just let it go with Plan C, or do Emergency Plan B? The father quickly called to mind that there was little to be gained by blowing his daughter's concern off the table. In fact, he didn't even know what her concern was! Nor his own! The father began with empathy.

"Helen, you want to sit on the register. What's up?"

"It's warmer," she replied.

"You want to sit on the register because it's warmer." The father now had to give serious thought to his own concern (if he really had one) and whether he wanted to put it on the table. If he decided he had no concern, of course, he would have simply chosen Plan C. I don't want your papers scattered all over the floor. Let's see if we can work this out. Do you have any ideas?"

"No, I want to sit here." Helen pouted.

"Oh, there must be a way to solve this problem," he prodded. "We've had tougher problems than this before. Let's think," the father encouraged.

"How 'bout I do my homework on the register tonight and at the kitchen table tomorrow night?" volunteered Helen.

"Well, that's an idea, but your papers would still be scattered all over the floor tonight," said the father. "Can you think of some other way for us both to be happy?"

"No, that's it!" Helen responded.

"There has to be some way for you to not be cold and for the papers not to be scattered all over the floor," the father said. "I have some ideas. Would you like to hear them?"

"Uhm . . . OK."

"We could turn up the heat so you wouldn't be cold . . . or you could put on a sweater . . . or we could find some way for your papers not to be scattered all over the floor. Any of those ideas work for you?"

"I think we should turn up the heat," said Helen.

"So we'll turn up the heat so you won't be cold, and then you won't need to sit on the register?"

"Yeah."

"Do you want me to help you move your things?"

"No, just go turn up the heat," said Helen.

"You did a very nice job of working things out," said the father.

In the next meeting with the family therapist, the father needed a little reassurance. "I'm afraid we're teaching her that she never has to listen to us, and I don't think that bodes well for the future."

"What, she never does what you tell her to now?" the therapist asked.

"No, she actually does what we ask quite often," he replied. "I'm worried that she'll think that all she has to do is start to throw a fit to get what she wants."

"You've been using Plan B for a few months now. Is she exploding less or more?" the therapist asked.

"A lot less." The father smiled.

"Is she meeting your expectations more or less?" the therapist asked.

"More," the father replied.

"Are you yelling a lot less?"

"Yes."

"How are you and Helen getting along lately?" the therapist asked.

"It's a lot better. You know, Helen was always a very affectionate kid. But we were battling so much that, up until a few weeks ago, when I'd get home from work, she'd barely even acknowledge my presence. For the past two weeks, when I get home from work, she jumps up from whatever she's doing and gives me a big hug."

"I think we're doing OK," the therapist said.

"But what about the real world?" the father asked.

"What about it?" the therapist asked.

"The real world doesn't have Plan B or people who always try to understand," he said.

"I don't expect that your fighting with her a lot will help her live in the real world. On the other hand, I do expect that helping her stay calm enough to think clearly in the midst of frustration will be very helpful to her in the real world. If you think about what the real world demands, it's a whole lot more about resolving disputes and disagreements than it is about blind adherence to authority."

7

Learning Curves

In Chapter 6, you learned about your three options for responding to problems or unmet expectations, and a lot in particular about one of the three options: Plan B. You were also given your first homework assignments: (1) make a list of the triggers that are routinely causing explosions, and (2) start solving problems using Proactive Plan B.

How did your first attempts at Plan B go? If your answer is "Not so bad," that's great. Now let's hope the solution you agreed to in Plan B stands the test of time. (If the solution doesn't durably solve the problem, you'll find out soon enough. Then it's back to Plan B to figure out why and come up with a solution that is more realistic, doable, or mutually acceptable than the first one.) And when you think the time is right, move on to another problem on the list.

But if your answer is "Not well at all," don't despair. In the last chapter, the numerous factors that could cause Plan B to go astray were discussed, including:

- *You may be overrelying on Emergency Plan B*. Remember, most explosions are highly predictable and should therefore be handled using Proactive Plan B. With Emergency Plan B, there's added heat and therefore lower odds.

- *You may be using Plan B as a last resort*. Plan B isn't an act of desperation, and it's not something you turn to only when your child is on the verge of exploding.

- *You may be putting solutions on the table instead of concerns*. Don't forget—the problem won't get solved unless two highly specific concerns are on the table.

- *You may be entering Plan B discussions with preordained solutions*. It's fine to have some ideas, but if you already know what the solution is before the discussion begins, you're using Plan A, not Plan B.

- *You may be agreeing to solutions that aren't realistic, doable, and mutually satisfactory*. Better to keep talking now than to agree on a solution that's only going to precipitate an explosion later.

- *You're feeling like you're not very good at Plan B yet, so you've been using a lot of Plan C instead and have been feeling as if your concerns aren't being addressed*. By definition, your concerns won't be addressed with Plan C. No one is great at Plan B in the beginning. You and your child are getting good at this together.

- *You're feeling as if you're not very good at Plan B yet, so you're still using a lot of Plan A instead*. Remember empathy (not "no") is the first step of Plan B. Empathy, not "no." Then do the remaining two steps.

But the most common reason things don't go well with Plan B is missing steps. You're not using Plan B unless you're doing the three steps in the prescribed order:

1. *Empathy (plus Reassurance)*
2. *Define the Problem*
3. *Invitation*

You may be routinely skipping a step. Let's take a closer look.

EMPATHY

If you skip the Empathy step, your child will think you're using Plan A because you're leading off with your concern and that's usually a signal that you're about to impose your will. The Empathy step keeps your child calm, gets his concern on the table, and reminds him that you're trying to do things differently.

A mother arrived at the counselor's office one day with a familiar complaint.

"Plan B isn't working," she said.

"Tell me the story," said the counselor.

"Well," said the mother, "on Tuesday I told Jeremy that I wanted to make sure he got his homework done before his karate class and asked him how we could work that out."

"So your concern was that he wouldn't get his homework done before his karate class," said the counselor.

"Right. I know that if he doesn't do his homework before his karate class, it's not going to get done because by the time we get home from his karate class he's too tired."

"That makes sense," said the counselor. "And what was it that you were trying to work out?"

"What were we trying to work out?" asked the mother, a little confused. "How we were going to get his homework done before his karate class."

"What was Jeremy's concern?" asked the counselor.

"His concern?" asked the mother, still confused.

"Yes, at the moment I'm hearing only your concern, which is that you were worried that he wouldn't get his homework done, and your solution, which is that he do his homework before karate class. What was his concern?"

"I didn't know he had a concern," said the mother.

"I'm wondering if that's because you skipped the first step of Plan B . . . empathy," the counselor said.

"I knew I was doing something wrong!" said the mother.

"No one does very well at this in the beginning," said the counselor. "What happened when you told him your concern and invited him to solve the problem with you?"

"He started screaming at me," said the mother.

"Sounds like he must have had a concern," said the counselor. "The problem is, when you skip the empathy part and jump right to your concern, he thinks you're using Plan A."

"So what should I have said?" asked the mother.

"Well, do you have any ideas about what concern he might have had about doing his homework before his karate class? Has this come up before?"

"Oh, it comes up all the time," said the mother. "He says he needs a break before he does his homework."

"Why does he need a break?" asked the counselor.

"Well, he's been in school all day—this is what he says—to tell you the truth, I don't know how hard he's actually

working in school. Anyway, he always seems to have enough energy for karate . . ."

"But I suppose it makes some sense that if he's been in school for six hours, he might need a break before he jumps right into homework," said the counselor. "Sounds like a valid concern to me, if that's what his concern actually is."

"I suppose so," conceded the mother.

"So let's think of what empathy might have sounded like," said the counselor. "What could you have said if you wanted to start Plan B off with empathy? Let's assume you're doing Proactive Plan B."

"Uhm . . . you mean something like, 'You're tired when you get home from school'?" the mother volunteered.

"That's a start," said the counselor. "Then you can follow the empathy with your concern. See, then you've actually got a problem to solve. Remember, you don't have a problem to solve until you've got two concerns on the table."

"This is hard!" said the mother.

"It takes a little getting used to. But we don't want you to miss out on the good stuff empathy brings to the mix. It keeps him calm and it gets his concern on the table."

"So how would we have solved the problem?" asked the mother.

"I don't know how you would have ultimately solved the problem. That's between you guys, but I'm betting there are lots of possibilities. Of course, we don't uncover those possi-

bilities unless we're doing Plan B. Have a Proactive Plan B discussion with him this week and see if he has any ideas about how you guys could solve that problem before it comes up again—once and for all?"

DEFINE THE PROBLEM

You might think that this step wouldn't often go missing since adults usually know what their concerns are. The reality is that adults often don't know what their concerns are—they know what their solutions are. It's actually quite common that adults have never really given much consideration at all to what their concerns are.

A ten-year-old boy went to summer camp for two months. The family therapist anticipated that the boy and his parents would be happier than usual when they came in for their first session after he came home from camp (since they hadn't seen one another for two months). But what walked into the office were three livid people.

"What's up?" the therapist asked no one in particular once the three were seated in the office.

"They won't give me my money," the boy seethed.

"What money?" asked the therapist.

The boy growled, "They put two months of allowance

into the camp canteen so I'd have money to spend at camp. I didn't spend all of the money they put into the canteen. NOW I WANT MY MONEY BACK!"

This sounded like a pretty specific concern, so the therapist turned to the father and asked, "What do you think?"

The father replied, "Over my dead body."

The therapist pondered what Plan "Over my dead body" was. Having quickly concluded that the father was using Plan A, the therapist tried to help the father articulate his concern more specifically. "What's your concern about that, Mr. Tremblay?"

"My concern is that Kyle's not getting his money back!" said the father.

Kaboom. *The next ten minutes were fairly unpleasant. The therapist was finally able to convince the boy to leave the office, whereupon she looked at the father and asked the million-dollar question: "I'm assuming you meant to be doing Plan A, yes?"*

"What makes you think that?" the father responded, a little puzzled.

"Well, if you had been doing Plan B, you would have tried to work it out; and if you were trying to do Plan C, you would have just given him the money," the therapist said. "You said 'Over my dead body,' which sounded very much like a 'no' to me."

"Oh, I don't care if he gets the money," the father replied.

"So what's your concern?" asked the therapist.

"My concern? What do you mean, my concern?"

"Your concern—you know, whatever's making you say 'Over my dead body.' "

"I don't like the tone he was using," said the father.

"Does Kyle know that's your concern?" the therapist asked.

"I don't know," said the father. "Why?"

"Because if your concern isn't on the table, or if it's not specific enough, Kyle will have no idea what problem you guys are trying to solve—and neither will you."

INVITATION

Many adults manage to get through the first two steps of Plan B and therefore get two concerns on the table. But then they dictate the solution and are faced with an explosion anyway. (In the words of the song, "So close . . . so close and yet so far away.") Sometimes this is because the adults still can't fathom that a child might be able to come up with a realistic, doable, and mutually satisfactory solution; but most often, it's just a bad habit.

The mother of a nine-year-old boy named Chuck arrived at the therapist's office for an appointment one April day and was extremely exasperated.

"What's up?" the therapist asked.

"He just exploded in the car," she responded.

"Over what?"

"He wants caps for his cap gun," she replied. "Can you imagine? An explosion over caps?"

"I can imagine," the therapist said. "Why did he explode over caps?"

"He wants them today," she said, "and I don't have time to buy them today."

"So you don't object to his having caps for his cap gun," the therapist said.

"No, he can have all the caps he wants," she said. "I even tried to work things out with him!"

"Really, what was the solution?" the therapist asked expectantly.

"I told him I'd buy him the caps in June," she said.

"June?" asked the therapist.

"June," she said. "I told him he could have the caps in June."

"How did you come up with June?" the therapist asked.

"I don't know—it just came to me," she said.

"Uhm, I think you may have skipped a step," the therapist said.

"What do you mean?" she asked.

"Well, you got two concerns onto the table—he wants his caps today and you don't have time to buy them

today—but you never really invited him to solve the problem collaboratively."

"What would a good solution have been?" the mother asked.

"That's for you and Chuck to decide," the therapist said. "Something realistic, doable, and mutually satisfactory. Chuck's reaction tells us your solution wasn't mutually satisfactory."

"You think he can do this?" said the mother.

"I've seen him do it before," said the therapist. "But let's get Chuck in here and see," the therapist said.

Chuck came into the office. "I understand you want caps for your cap gun," the therapist said.

"Yeah, but she won't get them for me till June," he groused.

"I think your mom might be willing to work out a solution to that problem," the therapist said.

"That was the solution!" Chuck complained.

"No, I think your mom might really be willing to work it out," the therapist said. "Chuck, you want to buy caps today and your mom doesn't have time to buy them for you today. Can you think of a way to work that out?"

Chuck pondered the possibilities very briefly but then became a little agitated. "I can't think of a way to work it out!" he said, squirming on the couch.

"If you need my help figuring it out, I'm happy to assist," the therapist said. "Can you think of any ideas?"

"NO!" Chuck screamed. "How 'bout May?" he pleaded in desperation.

"May could be a very good solution," said the therapist. Chuck quickly calmed. Then, knowing full well what his response would be, the therapist asked, "When in May?"

Without missing a beat, Chuck said, "May first."

The therapist looked at the mother. "How would May first be for you?"

The mother pulled out her date book, leafed through to May 1, and said, "May first would be a fine day to buy caps."

Of course, there are other possible factors that are interfering with the successful implementation of Plan B. It's possible that your child is lacking some skills crucial for participating in Plan B. That's the topic of the next chapter. It's also possible that one or more of your child's pathways would be better addressed by medicine than by Plan B. That topic is covered in chapter 10.

In the meantime, you now have enough information about the CPS model to have lots of questions. So let's answer some.

When is my child going to be held accountable for his actions?

For many folks, "Hold the child accountable" is code for "punishment." Many people believe that if the consequences a child has already received for his explosions haven't caused him to stop exploding, it must be because the punishments didn't cause the child enough pain. So they add more pain. The majority of explosive kids have had more pain than most people experience in a lifetime. If pain was going to work, it would have worked a long time ago. And you now know the things reward and punishment programs do well: They teach basic lessons well and they motivate well. It is the premise of this book that your child already knows you don't want him to explode and is already motivated not to explode. Mission accomplished. The notion that the only thing these kids need is a good kick in the butt is simply wrong and doesn't do justice to the diverse mechanisms that may underlie a child's difficulties. Indeed, a lot of the so-called explanations for their behavior are simply clichés that have little meaning once you think about them a while:

- *"He just wants attention."* We all want attention. So "he just wants attention" can't possibly explain why he's exploding.

- *"He just wants his own way."* We all want our own way. So that couldn't possibly explain why he's exploding.

- *"He just wants control."* We all want control. Same deal.

- *"He won't cooperate."* If you're talking about the true meaning of the word *cooperate*—"to collaborate, to come together"—then it's a pretty sure bet you've never given him the chance.

- *"He's manipulative."* I doubt it. Good manipulation requires forethought, planning, impulse control, organizational skills. Eighty percent of explosive kids are also diagnosed with ADHD. What are some of the core features of ADHD? Poor forethought, poor planning, poor impulse control, poor organizational skills. Explosive kids are typically very poor manipulators. They're bad at it. Competent manipulation is when you don't know you're being manipulated. If you know you're being manipulated, you're dealing with an incompetent manipulator.

- *"He just needs to step up to the plate."* How often do *you* step up to the plate when you're lacking the skills needed to hit the ball?

What's the CPS definition of holding a child accountable? *Give him the skills he needs so he doesn't explode anymore . . . and so he doesn't need your help anymore*. As long as your child is relying on your consequences as his motivation to not explode, he's not even close to being "held accountable." If you're not teaching a child the skills he needs to solve problems effectively and stop exploding, then you're not setting the stage for him to "be accountable."

So is my child "taking responsibility for his actions" when I'm using Plan B?

Yes. If your child is participating with you in Plan B discussions in an effort to solve the problems that cause him to behave maladaptively . . . if he's taking your concerns into account . . . if he's collaborating on solutions that are mutually acceptable . . . if he's exploding less . . . then he's "taking responsibility."

So Plan B isn't giving my child the message that I approve of his explosive behavior, right?

Plan A is not the only way to let your child know you disapprove of his behavior—he knows you disapprove when you put your concern on the table by doing Plan B (he probably knew you disapproved anyway). Don't forget the definition of limit setting: making sure your concerns are addressed. Since your concerns are being addressed with both Plan A and Plan B, you're setting limits in Plan B just as much as you're setting limits in Plan A—but in a very different way and with a completely different outcome.

What about the real world? What if my child has a Plan A boss someday?

A Plan A boss is a problem to be solved. How does your child learn problem-solving skills? Plan B. As discussed elsewhere, which skill is more important for life in the real world: the blind adherence to authority taught with Plan A or learning how to work things out with people, as taught with Plan B? Your humble author picks Door Number Two.

For example, a speed limit is an expectation, and there are Plan A reasons for not speeding and Plan B reasons for not speeding. The Plan A reason for not speeding is that you might get caught and have to pay a fine. The Plan B reasons for not speeding? You don't want to die. You don't want to kill someone else. You don't want your children to grow up without you. If the only reason you're not speeding is that you might get caught and have to pay a fine, then there's a pretty good chance you'll be speeding if there's some assurance you won't get caught (Exhibit A: the popularity of radar detectors). In which case you (and the rest of us) are still completely dependent on others (the police) to keep you in line. But if you're not speeding because you don't want to die, or you don't want to kill someone else, or you don't want your children to grow up without you, then it's your *thinking* that keeps you from speeding, thinking about the likely outcomes of, and who else is likely to be affected by, your behavior. This type of thinking is taught with Plan B. A child raised with Plan A is still completely dependent on adults (or other authority figures) to tell him what to do and make sure he does it.

Are safety issues best addressed with Plan A?

In previous variants of the CPS model, safety was addressed with Plan A. Now it's barely addressed with Plan A. Why? Because problems that cause children to be unsafe don't get solved with Plan A; they get solved with Plan B. Of course, if you see your child doing something unsafe (for example, darting into the path of a moving car in a parking lot), it's time for Plan A. Grab his arm, save his life, and if he explodes, so be it. But if you've noticed that he's chronically darting into the path of moving cars and you're chronically grabbing his arm to save his life, Plan A is clearly not getting the job done. Time for Proactive Plan B:

Parent (Empathy): Clark, I've noticed that it's a little hard for you to stay next to me when we're in parking lots. And then we get mad at each other because I have to grab you. You know what I mean?

Clark: Yup.

Parent (Define the Problem): The thing is, I can't let you run in front of cars because I don't want you to get hurt. Right?

Clark: Yup.

Parent (Invitation): Let's think of how we can solve that problem. Do you have any ideas?

Clark: Uhm . . . we could not go into parking lots.

Parent: There's an idea. The thing is, sometimes we have to go into parking lots—like to go food shopping or to go to the drugstore. So I don't know if we can stay away from parking lots completely. But I bet there's some way we could be in parking lots without me having to worry about you running in front of cars. What do you think?

Clark: You could leave me home with Grammy.

Parent: I could . . . sometimes. But Grammy can't always look after you when I'm out doing errands.

Clark: I could hold your hand.

Parent: You could hold my hand. I think that idea could work very well. But sometimes you get mad when I want to hold your hand in the parking lot.

Clark: That's 'cuz you're screaming at me.

Parent: I'm screaming at you because you're—uhm—you know what? If you and I agree that you're going to hold my hand in the parking lot from now on, then it won't matter why I was screaming at you.

Clark: What if I forget to hold your hand?

Parent: I'll try to remind you before we get there.

Clark: What if you forget not to scream at me?

Parent: I'm going to try very hard not to. If I slip, can you remind me?

Clark: Yup.

Parent: This plan work for you?

Clark: Yup.

Parent: It works for me, too. Thanks for solving the problem with me, buddy.

Of course, when parents say "safety issues," they're frequently referring to what their child is doing in the midst of an explosion (hitting, throwing things, etc.). But since most explosions are precipitated by an adult doing Plan A, there's a simple antidote: *Don't do Plan A in the first place.*

A mother was very upset that her son had punched her as they argued over whether he could eat five chocolate chip cookies. She was understandably very upset over having been hit. Her story suggested that there was work to be done on achieving safety. But her story also suggested that the mother had more work to do on her decision-making about the Plans.

"Hitting is Plan A, right?" the mother asked.

"How do you mean?" the therapist asked.

"If he hits me, then it's time for Plan A, right?" she asked.

"Well, I'm more concerned about what it was that caused him to hit you," the therapist responded. "What Plan did you want to use to address the chocolate chip cookie issue?"

The mother paused. "I didn't want him to have more chocolate chip cookies."

"So you told him he couldn't have any more," said the therapist.

"Right," said the mother.

"So you wanted to be using Plan A, yes?"

"What, you think I should have just let him eat the cookies?" asked the mother.

"Well, that would have been Plan C," said the therapist.

"So you're saying I should have been doing Plan B," said the mother.

"If you didn't want him to have five cookies and you didn't want him to explode, then yes, then Plan B would have been the way to accomplish those two missions simultaneously."

"You don't think him hitting me is serious?" asked the mother.

"Him hitting you is very serious," said the therapist.

"So what should I do about the hitting?" asked the mother.

"If you're solving problems and resolving disagreements with Plan B, I think you'll greatly reduce the likelihood of getting hit," said the therapist.

So what should I do if my child actually does explode?

If your child is exploding, it's a pretty sure bet you're doing Plan A. Stop! If you're lucky, your child is, at that moment, still capable of Plan B. If not, head for the Plan C hills. If you end up using Plan C, does that mean your child will learn that he need only to explode to get his way? Not if you do Proactive Plan B at your next opportunity to solve the problem that caused him to explode in the first place. If you have to endure an explosion, don't let it go to waste. Explosions provide very important information about pathways or triggers you may have missed. But that's the only productive thing about explosions: They give you the information you need to prevent another explosion over the same issue.

I don't have time to do Plan B. It takes too long.

You don't have time *not* to do Plan B! Explosions always take longer than Plan B. Unsolved problems always take more time than solved problems. Doing something that isn't working always takes more time than doing something that is working. And if you're doing a lot of Proactive Plan B—solving problems with durable solutions—then the amount of time you're spending doing Plan B should decrease as problems are solved.

I'm not that quick on my feet. I can't always decide what Plan to use on the spur of the moment.

All the more reason for you to be solving problems proactively rather than emergently. It's only with Emergency Plan B that you have to be real quick on your feet. If you find yourself in an emergent situation and you can't decide what Plan to use, your default option is Plan B.

By the way, some children will tolerate the uncertainty of a delayed Plan decision for a few minutes while their parents sort through the three options. In other words, it's not always critical that a decision be made immediately. If you think your child can handle a brief delay, you can say something like, "I need to think about whether I have any concerns about that. Can you give me a minute?" Other parents feel the need to delay a Plan decision because they'd prefer not to have such a dialogue in the car, supermarket, or shopping mall (places where their capacity to deal with their child's worst—if it happens—may be compromised).

A mother came in for a session one night hoarse from all the screaming she'd been doing at her daughter on the drive to the therapist's office.

"What were you screaming about?" the therapist asked.

"Alycia was very upset that we're going to have to change our plans for her birthday," she replied.

"That must have been very upsetting to her. But why all the screaming?" the therapist asked.

"Because it was foggy out, and I'm not the best at driving at night to begin with, and I've got a frustrated daughter sobbing in the backseat telling me I don't love her," she replied.

"What did you do?" the therapist asked

"I screamed at her," said the mother. "And now I'm sitting here really mad at myself for doing it. I guess I get a little worked up when she gets worked up."

"What was your goal when she started getting upset?" the therapist asked.

"I have no idea," replied the mother. "I just wanted to get past the problem, be done with it."

"That's an interesting goal," the therapist said. "Because you have a daughter who's not very good at just getting past problems and being done with them."

"That's for sure," the mother agreed. "So what should my goal be?"

"I think one important goal is to think about whether the ideal time and place to have a discussion that's going to be frustrating to Alycia is in the car at night when it's foggy. In other words, whether it's at all likely a productive discussion could take place under those conditions. If you decide that scenario probably wouldn't set the stage for the discussion you need to have with her, you could try to delay the discus-

sion until the circumstances are more ideal. Do you think Alycia would have been able to delay the discussion?"

"She still would have cried in the backseat," the mother said.

"Well, we can't keep her from feeling what she legitimately feels about her birthday plans being changed. But we can give more thought to whether delaying the discussion has the potential to lead to a more productive outcome."

My husband won't do Plan B. Any advice?

There are a lot of adults out there who fear that their concerns won't be heard or addressed. So they head straight for Plan A when they have a concern. Why are there a lot of adults who fear that their concerns won't be heard or addressed? Because there are a lot of adults who were raised with Plan A as children and their concerns were neither heard nor addressed! Adults who are perpetuating the cycle by using Plan A to ensure that their concerns are heard and addressed often need to be reminded that their concerns will be heard and addressed with Plan B as well. Then they need guidance on doing Plan B well.

But my husband says Plan A worked for him.

Maybe it did. Lucky him. But apparently it's not working for his child. If his child is lacking important thinking skills, and if Plan A is simply causing explosions and hostility and misery, then it's hard to imagine why your husband would want to stick with something that's not working. Maybe he thinks his only other option is Plan C. We'll have to help him learn about that third option.

My child won't do Plan B. I'm trying to work things out, but he's not.

Make sure you read the next chapter. As mentioned above, there are a variety of factors that could be interfering with your child's ability to do Plan B. So it's not that he doesn't want to do Plan B, it's that he's lacking some of the skills required for doing it. You may have some additional skills to teach him.

But when I tell my kid what my concern is, he says he doesn't care. How can I do Plan B with someone who doesn't care?

Your child doesn't have to "own" your concern to collaborate on solving the problem. The truth is, most adults don't "own" many of the concerns of, for example, their significant other. They don't *really* care; they just don't *say* they don't really care. So your child doesn't have to care about your concern, but he does need to take your concern into account to solve the problem in a way that is mutually satisfactory.

Parent: Billy, I know that you like playing with your friends after school and that it's sometimes hard to stop to come in for dinner.

Billy: Yeah.

Parent: The thing is, it's really important to me that we eat dinner together as a family.

Billy: I don't care if we eat dinner together as a family.

Parent: Uhm . . . OK . . . maybe it's more important to me that we eat together than it is to you. But I'd still like to see if we can solve the problem. You want to keep playing with your friends, and I want us to eat dinner together as a family. Let's think about different ways we could solve that problem.

My child and I agree on a solution and then he won't do what he agreed to.

As you'll read in Chapter 8, that's usually a sign that the solution wasn't realistic, doable, or mutually satisfactory in the first place. Remember, Plan B isn't an exercise in wishful thinking. Both parties need to be able to follow through on the solution. If your child isn't following through, it's probably not because he won't but because he can't. Better work toward a solution that he can actually do.

I've been taught that it's important for parents to be consistent with each other in front of the child so the child can't do any "splitting." So what advice do you give parents if one is using Plan A on an issue and the other disagrees?

Explosions are far more destructive to families than parents disagreeing in front of their children. What's interesting is that if two parents share the same concern, they already agree on the main point (that they have a concern to put on the table). Your concern is entered into consideration with both Plan A and Plan B. So if one has begun heading toward the point of no return (Plan A), good teamwork means that the other parent should jump in (quickly) and get the child's concern on the table (to initiate Plan B), head off an explosion, and get the problem solved. Then the parents need to talk privately about how they can get their concerns addressed without causing explosions.

Life is a bit more interesting if one parent is using Plan A and the other is doing Plan C, for this suggests that the parents are not yet in agreement about whether they should be putting a concern on the table. Before the issue is raised with the child, the parents need to discuss and agree upon whether the concern is actually worth pursuing.

For how long should I do Plan B? How much progress should I expect from my child, and how fast?

For how long should you do Plan B? Well, let's think about what you're doing. You're solving problems collaboratively with your child so you guys don't fight about those problems anymore. You're communicating with your child. You're improving your relationship. You're letting him know that you're not the only one with good ideas about how to solve problems, that he has good ideas, too. You're teaching him that his concerns are valid. Now why would you want to stop doing all that, even if he's not exploding anymore?

A lot of parents begin to use the approach described in this book thinking that eventually they'll be able to get back to Plan A again. In reality, as parents and children get better at Plan B and as their relationship improves, the importance of Plan A actually diminishes. Over time most parents don't miss Plan A, and they definitely don't long for the "good old days."

Children and parents vary widely in terms of how quickly they respond to this approach. The first goal is to take the fuel out of the fire as quickly as possible by dramatically decreasing the use of Plan A and dramatically increasing the use of Plans B and C. This shift in the way parents respond to and communicate with their child should correspond with a decrease in the frequency, duration, and intensity of explosions. And, of course, an increase in the use of Plan B also means that numerous triggers—problems that have yet to be solved—are getting solved. Some families are able to achieve this in a few weeks, some take several months, and others take longer still. Some children continue to have occasional, residual unsafe episodes for a few months, but such episodes are often far less intense and fizzle out a lot faster. As you'll read in the next chapter, once this phase has been reached, the stage is set for more direct work on your child's pathways.

Should I reward my child for doing Plan B?

Fewer explosions and getting along better with you are usually reward enough.

So, does using this approach mean that rewards and punishments are completely out of the picture?

Not necessarily. But by now you should have a very realistic sense of what rewards and punishments can and can't help you achieve and an awareness of the special care required when using consequences with an explosive child. The real question is this: Will additional motivation enhance your child's performance at any point along the way? The answer: probably not. But let's think about it.

The first thing you'd want to be convinced of is that your child actually needs additional motivation. Our philosophy, that children do well if they can, suggests that your child is already sufficiently motivated. Second, you'd want to be sure that motivational strategies are worth the potential price. Many an explosion has been precipitated by the delivery of a punishment or the loss of an anticipated reward.

Engaging children in discussions about how they can make amends for an act committed in the midst of frustration can be far more productive than punishment. Such discussions should not take place during or immediately after explosions but rather once rational thinking has been fully restored. Here's what such a discussion might sound like:

Parent: Carlos, we need to talk a little about the table you broke yesterday.

Child: I said I was sorry.

Parent: I know, and it was very nice of you to say that. But I still feel very bad about the broken table, and we still need to figure out what you can do to help me feel better.

Child: Like what?

Parent: I don't know. Can you think of anything you could do that would make me feel better?

Child: You could punish me.

Parent: I don't know if punishing you would make me feel better. And it certainly hasn't kept you from breaking things. I was thinking there might be some things you could help me with around the house.

Child: I could sweep the floors.

Parent: That's an idea. That would be very helpful. Is that something you'd do to help me feel better?

Child: Yes. Or I could help you take out the trash.

Parent: I think it would be most helpful for you to sweep the floors. That would make me feel a lot better. Maybe next time you get frustrated you could let me help you instead of breaking the table.

Child: I'll try.

What about time-out?

Some children actually find time-out to be a good place to calm down when they're frustrated, although this is the exception, since time-out is usually used as a punishment. More commonly, the explosions of many children are actually exacerbated—sometimes dramatically so—if someone makes any kind of physical contact with them when they're frustrated. So if time-out simply fuels your child's explosions, forget it. Even under optimal circumstances, time-out is typically not recommended for older children and adolescents.

On the other hand, it can be productive to help parents and children agree to go their separate ways—with each going to different designated rooms of the house—when it becomes obvious that a discussion is going poorly or is not going to be resolved immediately. Not all explosive children will follow through on this plan, but a surprising number will. The discussion resumes after everyone has calmed down and had a chance to think a little.

But I still have the feeling that some of my child's behavior is planned and willful. How do I tell the difference?

The last thing you'd want to try to do at times when your child is becoming frustrated is to quickly try to figure out whether his behavior is planned or unplanned. You don't have a whole lot of time to spare, and it isn't easy to tell. So there are essentially two possible mistakes you can make at such moments. The first is to think your child's behavior is unplanned and unintentional when it really isn't. The second is thinking your child's behavior is planned and intentional when it really isn't. If you have to make an error, make the first error. In other words, when in doubt, respond as if your child's behavior is unplanned and unintentional. The ramifications of the second error are much more serious.

My child becomes frustrated about things that don't involve interactions with me or other people. He just gets really frustrated with something he's doing, like playing PlayStation. Or sometimes he has a delayed response to a frustration that happened earlier in the day. What then?

It's true, there are times when it seems as if there's nothing to work out because your child's frustration didn't involve you or another person. And there are instances in which a child's frustration at the moment is a delayed response to an earlier frustration, such as something that happened in school. But your role remains the same: to find out what's up and help solve the problem (perhaps with Emergency B today, but with Proactive B tomorrow if the problem was really quite predictable).

Mother (standing on the front walk to the house): Charlotte, we're waiting for you to get in the car so we can go to the beach.

Charlotte (standing in the front doorway): I'm not going.

Mother: What? Charlotte, you love the beach.

Charlotte (backing into the house): I said I'm not going!

Mother (moving toward the front door, and using Plan A): Charlotte, your brother and father are already in the car, we're in a hurry, and I don't feel like going through this with you right now! Go get me my keys and let's go!

Charlotte (slamming and locking the front door to the house): Stay away from me! I'm not going!

Mother (still using Plan A): Charlotte, you unlock this door right now! (Turning to husband in car): Honey, do you have your keys?

Husband: No. Why?

Mother (pulse pounding, turning back to the locked front door, still using Plan A): Charlotte, open the door, dammit! This isn't funny!

[No response from inside the house.]

Father (arriving at front door): What's going on?

Mother (through gritted teeth): Your daughter has informed me that she's not going to the beach and has locked us out of our house.

Hmmm. That actually looks like an example of how *not* to do it. Now, through the magic of book writing, let's do something that you don't have the luxury of doing in real life: rewind the tape and try a different approach.

Charlotte: I'm not going.

Mother (Empathy, with a question mark): You're not going?

Charlotte: No, I'm not going!

Mother: What's the matter, honey?

Charlotte (rubbing her eyes): I just don't want to go.

Mother (squatting down to Charlotte's level): Is there something about going to the beach today that's bothering you? You usually can't wait to go to the beach.

Charlotte: It's too early to go to the beach!

Mother: I don't know what you mean that it's too early to go to the beach.

Charlotte: We don't usually go to the beach until after church. We never go to the beach in the morning.

Mother (Refined Empathy): It's bothering you that we don't usually go to the beach in the morning.

Charlotte: We never go to the beach in the morning. We can't go right now.

Mother (Defining the Problem): I'm glad you told me what was the matter. The thing is, we're all ready to go. But let's think about this a little. Maybe we can figure out what to do.

Much nicer.

My child has to have each solution spelled out in perfect detail. Is this normal?

Many explosive kids don't handle ambiguity in their lives well, and this extends to their solutions to problems.

So statements like "OK, we'll do that later" or "We'll go there soon" or "You can do that for a while" have the potential to fuel their frustration, even in the context of Plan B.

Trent (sitting in the backseat of the family car): I need something to eat.

Mother (in the role of genius and lucking out, temporarily): We'll stop for something very soon.

Trent: OK.

[Five minutes of silence elapse.]

Trent (with agitation): I thought you said we were stopping to eat!

Mother: I said we'd stop soon.

Trent (with significantly greater agitation): I can't wait! You said we were stopping!

Father (choosing Plan A over performing a rescue mission): Your mother said we'd stop soon; now put a lid on it!

Trent (very loudly, kicking the back of his father's seat): You guys are such freaking liars! You always do this! You say you'll do something, and then you don't!

Mother (still no Empathy): Look, we'll stop for food as soon as we can.

[*Kaboom.*]

On a related topic, some kids don't adapt well when a solution doesn't go exactly as planned. Mike, a remarkably rigid thirteen-year-old, had agreed with his mother over when (twelve noon on Saturday) and how (with her help) he'd clean his room. Mike was actually eager to get his room straightened up, but he lacked the organizational skills to do it on his own. Unfortunately, the mother was delayed by another commitment and wasn't around at twelve noon to help Mike clean his room. This change in plan proved to be a major obstacle for Mike. When the mother arrived home at 1:30 P.M. and suggested that they begin cleaning the room, Mike was very agitated. At 1:31 the mother insisted that they clean the room. Mike's agitation increased. The mother insisted further. At 1:32 Mike exploded. What Mike needed was a complete reconfiguring of the original solution. He was just that rigid.

Many of the examples I've read so far relate to younger children. My explosive child is fifteen. Any special suggestions?

Believe it or not, your child's chronological age is not the key issue. His developmental age in the domains of flexibility and frustration tolerance is the key issue. So while the language we'd use would probably be more sophisticated for a fifteen-year-old than for a four-year-old, the emphasis on identifying pathways and triggers would be exactly the same. Kids respond to being understood and to a collaborative approach regardless of age.

My explosive child has siblings who are nonexplosive and respond to Plan A. Am I supposed to have two different types of discipline going on in my household at the same time?

Kids who respond to Plan A also tend to respond to Plan B, so if you want to be consistent, do Plan B with your nonexplosive kids, too. But here's another angle: There isn't a household in the world where all the children are treated exactly the same. In all households, one child is getting something another isn't getting. Fair does not mean equal. Your nonexplosive children want your explosive child to stop exploding more than they want everyone to be treated exactly the same. More on siblings, though, in chapter 9.

How come my child explodes at home but not at school? Doesn't that prove he can hold it together when he feels like it?

Well, more likely it proves something we already knew: that he explodes only under certain conditions. Schools have a few advantages over homes. The schedule is more predictable (that's helpful for some explosive kids), there's less unstructured time (that's helpful for some explosive kids), and your child's medicine (especially if it's a stimulant) is in full effect during school hours. But the main advantage schools have is the embarrassment factor: Your child is keeping himself very tightly wrapped at school because he doesn't want to embarrass himself. Then he gets home and unravels because he's put so much energy into staying tightly wrapped at school. See, he can't keep himself tightly wrapped twenty-four hours a day. Homes aren't as structured and predictable as most schools, and homes don't have the embarrassment factor.

My child is exploding at school, and I don't think the teachers have heard of this model. Advice?

Sounds like your child is blowing through the embarrassment factor. Schools (not all but most) tend to be bastions of Plan A. You'll have to make sure they get exposed to this model. More in Chapter 11.

There are many problems that haven't been mentioned yet—like lying, stealing, drug use, sex—how would those problems be handled using Plan B?

The steps are the same, and the Empathy step may be the hardest. Just remember, some difficult issues require more than one Plan B conversation. Sometimes the solution that ends up solving the problem durably isn't arrived at until after a few solutions to the problem have been tried.

But here's what a Proactive Plan B conversation might look like on the lying issue:

Adult (Empathy): I've noticed that sometimes it's hard for you to tell me the truth about some things.

Child: Like what?

Adult: Well, the other day I asked you if your homework was done, and you told me it was. So I let you keep playing your video game. But I got a note from Mrs. Nixon today that your homework actually wasn't done.

Child: She's lying!

Adult (Empathy): She could be lying, I guess. But I've noticed that you were having trouble telling the truth about some other things that had nothing to do with Mrs. Nixon.

Child: What else?

Adult: Uhm, when I called home from my meeting last week I asked you if you had mowed the lawn, and you told me you had. And then I got home and the lawn wasn't mowed. Remember?

Child: Well, I meant to mow the lawn before you got home, but I didn't get to it.

Adult (Empathy, then Defining the Problem): I understand how that could happen. The thing is, when you lie to me about those things, it makes me feel like I can't trust you on other things.

Child: OK, I won't lie anymore!

Adult (Clarifying the Problem): Uhm, that would be wonderful. But I think I'd feel a little more confident about that if I understood why you were having trouble telling me the truth in the first place.

Child: I don't want you to get mad at me and punish me.

Adult (Empathy): Ah, you don't want me to get mad and punish you. I can understand that. I guess I can get pretty mad about things, can't I?

Child: Yup.

Adult (Redefining the Problem, then Invitation): OK, so you sometimes have trouble telling me the truth because you don't want me to get mad and punish you. And I want to feel like I can trust you to tell the truth. Let's think about what we can do about that. You have any ideas?

Child: You could promise not to get mad and punish me.

Adult: I could promise that. I'm trying very hard not to punish you anymore because it doesn't seem to be helping. Have you noticed?

Child: Sorta.

Adult: But I don't know if I can promise that I'll never get mad at you again. I might slip sometimes. I can promise to try very hard not to get mad at you.

Child: I could promise to try very hard not to lie to you.

Adult: So we both have something to work on, don't we?

Child: Yup.

Adult: What should we do if I slip up and get mad?

Child: I could remind you of your promise.

Adult: That would be very helpful. What should I do if you slip up and tell me a lie?

Child: You could remind me of my promise.

Adult: I think we've got a plan. Let's see how it works. If it doesn't work too well, we'll talk again and see if we can figure out what to do instead.

Child: OK.

What if you thought that your adolescent daughter was having unprotected sex with her boyfriend and you had some concerns about that? With Plan A you're starting the conversation by saying "You must not have sex with your boyfriend," in which case the conversation wouldn't take place because you ended the discussion before it even got started. With Plan C you're not having the conversation because you're not raising the topic. And here's what it looks like with Plan B:

Parent: Can we talk about something?

Daughter: Like what?

Parent: Like you and Kenny.

Daughter: Oh, no, here we go again.

Parent: No, wait—I just want to talk. I'm not going to lecture you.

Daughter: Yeah, right.

Parent: Look, I know you have very strong feelings for Kenny and you want to show him how you feel.

Daughter: I do not want to talk about this with you.

Parent: I know. This isn't exactly a walk in the park for me, either. But I'm concerned about you.

Daughter: Don't be, I'm fine.

Parent: I can't help it. Mothers worry about their daughters.

Daughter: Thank you for worrying about me. This is none of your business.

Parent: Can you just bear with me for one second? Even if it's none of my business.

Daughter: Fine. Talk. Fast.

Parent: Maybe we should find a better time to talk about it.

Daughter: There is no good time to talk about this! Talk! Before I change my mind!

Parent: OK. I know you have strong feelings for Kenny and you want to show him how you feel.

Daughter: You're repeating yourself.

Parent: Yes, I am. I'm worried that you're going to get pregnant.

Daughter: Oh, my God! I cannot believe we're talking about this! This is so embarrassing! I'm not going to get pregnant!

Parent: What's keeping you from getting pregnant?

Daughter: This is too embarrassing!

Parent: So reassure me a little so we can stop talking about it.

Daughter: Kenny uses condoms. I cannot believe this!

Parent: Always? Every time?

Daughter: Almost every time. Are we done?

Parent: Uhm . . . almost. Almost every time means you could still get pregnant.

Daughter: I'm not going to get pregnant!

Parent: I appreciate your confidence about that. I'm just wondering how we can make me more confident about that.

Daughter: It's not my job to make you more confident about that.

Parent: No, I guess it's not. But I do worry, and I'd like to not worry.

Daughter: Fine, stop worrying.

Parent: I wish it was that easy. Look, as long as we're on the topic, can we talk about one more thing?

Daughter: This conversation is taking too long already.

Parent: Should we talk about it another time?

Daughter: No, let's get this over with.

Parent: You don't think you're too young? Are you sure you can handle all the feelings that go along with it? What about your reputation?

Daughter: Look, Mom, I've been messing around with Kenny for longer than you know. I'm handling it. I love him. He loves me. My reputation is fine.

Parent: OK. Look, I just wanted to talk about those things—to make sure you were thinking about them. I didn't have sex with anyone when I was fifteen, and I didn't think my daughter would either.

Daughter: Sorry to disappoint you. But I'm really OK. It's nice of you to care. Sort of.

Parent: Well, I'm not completely convinced that you're OK, but I'll leave it alone for now. But if you're going to be doing it—and there's no way I can stop you, I guess—then can we at least make sure you're using a form of contraception that's a little more reliable?

I'm too tired to do this. I'm sick of my child and I don't have the energy to do all the talking and working things out that you've described. Any advice?

Living with an explosive child requires a lot of energy. Which means we've got to find ways to get you your energy back. I've seen the approach described in this book accomplish just that. As parents begin to understand their child's difficulties and respond in a more productive fashion, then the child begins to explode less. Then the parent starts to feel a greater sense of empowerment. As things continue to go well, the parent begins to feel more energized and optimistic.

But it's also the case that some parents need to focus on themselves (sometimes with a therapist), find ways to spend time away from the child and recharge, and find ways to focus on other aspects of life besides the child. Mental health clinicians, support groups, social service agencies, spouses, relatives, and friends can sometimes be of help.

8

Teach Your Children Well

We've covered a fair amount of ground already. At this point, I hope you have a sense of your child's pathways (skills that need to be taught) and have identified various triggers that routinely precipitate explosive outbursts (problems that need to be solved). Perhaps you've reduced some of the tension in your household by eliminating some unnecessary or unrealistic expectations (with Plan C). And perhaps you've reduced the likelihood of explosions even further by collaboratively solving some of the problems that were precipitating those explosions (with Plan B). Bear in mind that you may feel as if you're slogging through mud in your first attempts at Plan B. It can take a while to get into a Plan B rhythm.

However, as you've read, it's also the case that there are some specific skills that are necessary for a child to participate in Plan B discussions. As you'll see, these skills were already described when the pathways were reviewed in Chapter 3; now we need to put some thought into how these skills can be taught. We'll cover that topic next. And while we're at it, we should be sure to touch upon other skills reviewed in Chapter 3, just to make sure we've got all our bases covered.

SKILLS NEEDED TO PARTICIPATE IN PLAN B

There are three basic skills necessary for your child to participate in Plan B discussions. First, he must be able to *identify and articulate his concerns*. Otherwise, we won't be able to get two concerns onto the table and the Plan B ship won't leave port. Second, he needs to be able to *consider a range of possible solutions,* or the Plan B ship will run aground. Finally, he needs to be able to *reflect on the feasibility and likely outcomes of solutions and the degree to which they are mutually satisfactory*. Otherwise, the Plan B ship will chug in random directions, perhaps never arriving at a desired port. If your child is lacking these skills, you've got more work to do. Let's take 'em one at a time.

Identifying and Articulating Concerns

When you're trying to get your child's concerns on the table and you ask him "What's up?" there's a pretty good chance his response will be "I don't know." Does that mean Plan B is done for? No, but it does mean you have a skill to teach. Some kids truly don't know what their concern is; others don't have the language skills to articulate their concern. Luckily, because explosions are highly predictable—once again, your child is often exploding over many of the same problems or frustrations—we can probably take very educated guesses as to what your child is frustrated about.

Here's what a Proactive Plan B discussion would sound like if you were trying to help your child identify his concern:

Parent (Empathy): I've noticed you don't want to take your medicine anymore.

Child: Right.

Parent: What's up?

Child: I don't know.

Parent: You don't know why you don't want to take your medicine anymore?

Child: No. I just don't want to.

Parent: Well, I can think of a few reasons why someone wouldn't want to take their medicine. Should I guess? Then we can try to solve the problem.

Child: OK.

Parent: I've noticed that it seems to make you tired sometimes. Is that it?

Child: Well, it does make me a little tired, but I don't mind that so much.

Parent: OK, I guess that's not it. Is it that you're having trouble swallowing the pill? I've noticed that you don't seem to have an easy time with that.

Child: How could you tell?

Parent: Because it looks like you're about to choke before you finally swallow the pill.

Child: That's it.

Parent: That's it? You're having trouble swallowing the pill? That's why you don't want to take it?

Child: Yes.

Now that the child's concern has been identified and is on the table, the Plan B discussion can continue with the Define the Problem and Invitation steps, as described in Chapter 6.

Let's say that sensory hypersensitivities are a common trigger for your child. But while he's aware that, for example, tags in his clothing are bothersome, he's having difficulty verbalizing that concern. It would make sense to help your child articulate his concern—perhaps "The label is bothering me"—in order to circumvent the swearing, screaming, and thrashing about that normally accompanies this frustration. Here's how that might sound:

Parent: I've noticed that the labels in your clothing bug you a lot.

Child: Yeah.

Parent: And I've noticed that it's not so easy for you to say that the labels are bugging you.

Child: It's not?

Parent: Well, when the labels bother you, sometimes you scream or say some words that aren't very nice.

Child: Oh, yeah.

Parent: So, I was thinking that maybe we could come up with a way for you to say that the labels are bugging you without you saying words that aren't very nice. Can you think of any ideas for what you could say?

Of course, since children do well if they can, we'd have to assume that if the child already knew more appropriate words, he'd already be using them. So be prepared to offer a few suggestions:

Child: No.

Parent: I have an idea. Would you like to hear it?

Child: OK.

Parent: How about "The label's bothering me"?

Child: Uhm . . . OK.

Parent: Do you think you might be able to say that when the label's bothering you instead of some of the things you usually say?

Child: I think so.

Parent: If you forget, how about I remind you?

Incidentally, by merely raising the issue, you've let the child know that you don't think his choice of words is appropriate (of course, he probably knew that already). Naturally, your child's new vocabulary won't be ingrained in one day. He'll almost certainly need some in-the-moment reminders:

Child: I hate this shirt! It sucks!

Parent: Uh-oh . . . looks like the label is bugging you.

Note that the parent isn't reminding by saying "Don't forget what we agreed on yesterday" or "You can't talk to me that way," because these aren't specific enough reminders of the new vocabulary.

Of course, "The label is bothering me" is a highly specific phrase. It applies only to situations in which labels are bothersome. So it's often productive to teach a more general set of phrases that can be applied across many different situations. We adults greatly overestimate our own vocabularies when it comes to articulating frustrations. The truth is, we're usually relying on just a few reliable expressions. Phrases you might want to consider teaching your child include "*Gimme a minute,*" "*I can't talk about that right now,*" "*I need help,*" "*I don't feel right,*" "*This isn't going the way I thought it would,*" and "*I don't know what to do.*" Teaching these phrases looks exactly the same as the "labels" phrase above. And it's a sure bet some gentle reminding will be necessary on these phrases as well.

Mother: Jackson, how was your day at school?
Jackson: DON'T ASK ME THAT QUESTION?!!! SHUT UP!!!
Mother: Sounds like you can't talk about that right now.
Jackson: I CAN'T TALK ABOUT THAT RIGHT NOW!
Mother: No problem, maybe you'll be able to talk about it later.

How quickly will your child reliably use this new vocabulary? Hard to say. But if this is the skill your child is lacking, this is the way to teach it.

Considering a Range of Possible Solutions

As you know, the third step of Plan B is the Invitation. This is the step where you and your child are brainstorming potential solutions to the problem (defined by the two concerns that were put on the table in the first two steps). As you read in Chapter 6, if your child is unable to think of any solutions, that's a clear sign that he's, well, having trouble thinking of solutions. Of course, it could be a sign that you've never given him the chance to think of solutions. So it's possible that your child's skills in this area are better than you think. If his solution-generating skills aren't so hot, it's possible that they will improve simply by hearing you propose potential solutions numerous times.

But some kids truly don't have the slightest idea where to start when it comes to thinking of solutions. So let's give them an idea of where to start. Hard to believe, but it turns out that the vast majority of solutions to problems encountered by human beings fall into one of three general categories: *(1) ask for help; (2) meet halfway/ give a little;* and *(3) do it a different way*. These categories can be very helpful to children whose pathways are in the language-processing domain, for they simplify the language of problem solving and can be taught through pictures (if words are too cumbersome). The categories can also be helpful to children who become easily overwhelmed by the universe of potential solutions. First you'll want to introduce the categories to your child at an opportune moment; then, when you're trying to generate solutions using Plan B, use the categories as the framework for considering solutions:

Parent: I've noticed that you haven't wanted to go to gymnastics lately. What's up?

Child: I don't like my new coach.

Adult: You don't like your new coach. You mean Ginny? How come?

Child: It's boring. All she has us do is stretch. That's boring.

Adult: OK, let me make sure I've got this straight. You haven't wanted to go to gymnastics lately because it's boring . . . just a bunch of stretching.

Child: Right.

Adult: I can understand that. The thing is, you usually really like gymnastics, and you're really good at it, so I'd hate to see you give it up.

Child: I don't care.

Adult: Really? You sure you don't care?

Child: Not if it's just going to be a bunch of stretching.

Adult: Well, I wonder if there's a way to solve this problem so you're doing more of the things you like in gymnastics.

Child: Ginny's not going to change the way she does her class.

Adult: You might be right about that. But let's think about this. I don't know if "asking for help" will solve this problem. And I can't think of how we would "meet halfway" or "give a little" on this one, especially if you think Ginny isn't going to change the way she does her class. I'm thinking this is one where we'd "try to do it a different way." What do you think?

Child: I don't know what a different way would be.

Adult: Well, Ginny's not the only one who teaches that level. The main reason we picked Ginny's class is because the other class that's your level is the same time as your ice skating lesson. But I bet we could change ice skating to a different time. Then you could be in the other class. What do you think?

Naturally, this Plan B discussion would continue until a realistic, doable, and mutually satisfactory solution has been agreed upon. Not only would the problem get solved, Plan B would have been done in a way that set the stage, over time, for the child to begin using the categories as a framework for generating solutions. The expectation is that eventually the child would no longer need a "surrogate frontal lobe" to steer her through the process.

Reflect on the Likely Outcomes of Solutions and the Degree to Which They Are Feasible and Mutually Satisfactory

One of the reasons parents lose faith in Plan B—at least initially—is that the child has failed to follow through on an agreed-upon solution. As you know, this is usually the sign of an unrealistic solution (one of the two parties involved wasn't actually capable of delivering on what they'd agreed to) or a solution that failed to adequately address the child's concern. Remember, Plan B isn't an exercise in wishful thinking; it's the hard work of collaborating on mutually satisfactory and doable solutions.

It turns out that a lot of children (perhaps especially those whose difficulties involve the executive skills pathway) have difficulty thinking about the likely outcomes of solutions they consider. Others (often those whose difficulties involve the cognitive flexibility skills and social skills pathways) have difficulty thinking about whether the solutions under consideration are truly realistic and address both concerns. The first issue can be addressed by having the surrogate frontal lobe anticipate and describe the likely outcomes of the solutions that have been generated. ("Well, here's what I think will happen if we choose that solution, and here's what I think it will look like if we choose the second option.

Which of those outcomes do you think would work the best?") If a child is having difficulty thinking about whether solutions address both concerns, adults can respond as follows: "Miguel, I know that solution would make you happy, but it wouldn't make me very happy. Let's try to think of a solution that would make *both* of us happy." If the child can't think of a mutually satisfactory solution, the surrogate frontal lobe is there to help. After multiple repetitions the child should be better able to independently generate solutions that are mutually satisfactory.

TRAINING OTHER SKILLS WITH PLAN B

Language Processing Skills

Some of the skills discussed above can emanate from difficulties in language processing. But, as you read in Chapter 3, there are a few other language processing skills worth thinking about as they relate to your child's ability to deal effectively with frustration. Some children, for example, have trouble expressing the fact that they're frustrated. In other words, they lack a basic vocabulary of feeling words, so they don't have the words to tell you that they're frustrated. Instead, they swear or hit or destroy things.

So if a child is lacking a basic vocabulary of feeling

words, there's only one thing to do: Teach him a basic vocabulary of feeling words, starting with *happy, sad,* and, of course, *frustrated*. Why only three words? Because—regardless of a person's age—if you're overambitious in teaching new skills you won't teach any skills at all. And because those three feelings cover about 80 percent of human emotions anyway. Once a child becomes comfortable with and begins using this rudimentary vocabulary, more sophisticated feeling words—despondent, dysphoric, disenfranchised, discombobulated—can be added to a child's repertoire.

For some kids, even starting with the word *frustrated* is too advanced. Some actually can't say the word, in which case "angry" or "mad" will suffice. For some, saying *any* words is too frustrating, in which case it's often useful to have the child point to a picture of a frustrated face or rank their level of frustration with numbers, a 0 to 5 ranking system, in which 0 denotes "not frustrated at all" and 5 denotes "really, really frustrated"; or colors, for example, green denotes "not frustrated at all," yellow signifies "starting to get frustrated," and red denotes "really, really, frustrated." Of course, it's important for the adults to use the same terminology as the child and to give the child opportunities for using the language at times other than when he's most frustrated.

For example, Helen—a child you read about in Chapter 4—learned and practiced her rudimentary vocabulary by discussing the past day's events with her parents at bedtime. The parents would ask her what happened during the day that made her happy, whether anything made her sad, and whether anything caused her to feel frustrated. If Helen couldn't remember specific events that fit one of these three categories, her parents would suggest some possibilities. If Helen had difficulty labeling the emotions that were associated with a particular event, her parents would help her. The parents made sure Helen's teacher was also aware of her new vocabulary so that Helen didn't become confused by different terminology. When Helen became frustrated and expressed her frustration inappropriately ("No! I can't do that right now!" "Leave me alone!" "Screw you!" or worse), her parents and teacher would calmly remind her of her new vocabulary ("Boy, you sure sound frustrated!"). Over the course of several months Helen began to express her emotions in a much more appropriate manner across an increased number and range of situations. And her vocabulary of emotions slowly became broader and more sophisticated and eventually included such terms as confused, disappointed, excited, bored, and annoyed.

Don't forget: Just as a child with a reading disability won't begin reading overnight, a child (explosive or not) who has difficulty recognizing, expressing, or describing frustration won't begin using his new vocabulary overnight. There's no quick fix. But this isn't rocket science, either. The skills we're teaching are fairly basic. It's just that consequences don't teach them.

So if swearing is usually a sign that a child doesn't currently have the linguistic skills to express frustration adaptively, then responding to swearing with "I refuse to be spoken to like that!" or "Go to your room and come back when you're ready to talk to me the right way!" wouldn't get the job done (unless your child actually lacked the knowledge that you didn't want to be spoken to that way or wasn't motivated to speak to you the right way).

Mother: We had a bad incident this week, and I'm not sure I handled it well.

Therapist: Tell me.

Mother: Well, I was making pancakes for breakfast. Derrick came into the kitchen and said he didn't want pancakes. I told him that's what was on the menu—

Therapist: Sorry to interrupt, but did you mean to be handling eating pancakes with Plan A?

Mother (smiling): No.

Therapist: Just curious. Go on.

Mother: So then he called me a name and ran out of the kitchen. I ran after him and told him he was grounded for a week for calling me a name. He told me to get away from him. I insisted on an immediate apology. He went ballistic for the next half hour.

Therapist: It sounds extremely unpleasant. You mentioned that you wished you'd handled things differently?

Mother: First off, I shouldn't have been doing Plan A on the pancakes—I could have helped him find something else to eat.

Therapist: True. You could have done that with Plan B or C. Anything else?

Mother: I guess I shouldn't get so upset when he swears at me.

Therapist: It's very hard not to get upset when your son calls you a name. But you've been punishing him for calling you names for a very long time, and he still calls you a name every time he gets frustrated. So I don't think he needs any more lessons on the importance of not swearing or any more motivation not to swear. At the moment, it seems pretty clear that Derrick isn't very good at expressing his frustration without swearing. So he needs your help.

Mother: So what should I have said?

Therapist: Did you have a concern to put on the table? Besides the swearing, I mean.

Mother: Uhm . . . well, I wasn't dying to make him something else . . . you know, we were in a bit of a rush. But it's not like he would have wanted me to make him an omelet! No, I guess I really didn't have a concern.

Therapist: Then you'd have handled it with Plan C, in which case you could have said, "I think what you're saying is that you'd like something else to eat besides pancakes. What would you like?"

Mother: So I blew it, right?

Therapist: No, you didn't blow it . . . this is really hard. Your understandable knee-jerk instinct is to punish your kid when he swears at you, and I'm asking you to do something different because punishing him isn't working. It's hard to do.

Mother: Yes, it is. How will he learn that swearing's not OK?

Therapist: First of all, I think he knows swearing's not OK. He swears under only one condition: when he's frustrated. If he thought swearing was OK, he'd be swearing at other times, too. But even if he did think swearing was OK, you're still letting him know it's not by giving him different words to use. I think it's worth pointing out that Derrick did something very adaptive in the incident you described.

Mother: He did? What?

Therapist: Instead of going toe-to-toe with you in the kitchen, he detached himself from the situation. In other words, he left. He went into the other room. That's something he would never have done before. But you followed him.

Mother: I did, didn't I.

Therapist: So we have some more work to do. But we're getting there.

For children with linguistic impairments, language therapists can also be very helpful at facilitating many of the pragmatic skills discussed in this and the preceding chapter; specifically, helping children label their emotions, identify and articulate their frustrations, and think through solutions.

Executive Skills

Let's think back on some of the executive skills reviewed in chapter 3: *organization and planning, shifting cognitive set*, and *separation of affect*. How does Plan B address difficulties a child might be having in these domains? Well, Plan B provides your child with an organized, structured, predictable framework for solving problems and helps him consider a range of possible solutions (besides the first thing that pops into his head) and anticipate the likely outcomes of alternative solutions. Proactive B can help you and your child solve the predictable problems that arise with respect to the shifts or transitions that are required throughout the day in your household (for example, from sleeping to waking, getting dressed to eating breakfast, eating breakfast to catching the bus, school to home, free time to homework, and TV time to dinner or bedtime). And of all the things Plan B does well, helping your child suspend his emotional response to a problem so that he can stay calm enough to think (separation of affect) would be high on the list. Many children who have difficulties with executive skills are also hyperactive and/or inattentive, and, as described in Chapter 10, these children may also be helped by medication.

Emotion Regulation Skills

As you read in Chapter 3, kids who have difficulties regulating their emotions are often more irritable or anxious than other kids. And, as you also read, irritability and anxiety can make it hard for any of us to think clearly under duress. There is a very strong tendency (especially in the United States) to use medication to reduce children's irritability and anxiety, and for some children medication is truly indispensable. But one reason such medications are overused is that a lot of prescribers don't know about the pathways and haven't really gotten to the bottom of a child's irritability or anxiety. Can Plan B reduce a child's anxiety and irritability? Absolutely—by helping parent and child solve the problems that are contributing to the irritability and anxiety in the first place. In other words, many children's irritability and anxiety can be traced back to chronic problems that have perpetually gone unsolved. Might the child be less anxious if we finally found a way to solve the problem of the monster under the bed? Might the child's anxiety be reduced and mood be enhanced if the problem of being bullied at school was finally durably solved? If the problem of an unrecognized learning disability that has been adversely affecting his academic performance was finally durably solved? If his father's alcoholism was finally acknowledged and addressed? Medicine doesn't solve these problems, and neither do consequences. Only solving problems solves problems.

Cognitive Flexibility Skills.

As you may recall, children whose difficulties stem from the cognitive flexibility pathway typically approach the world in a very black-and-white, literal, rigid manner. They have difficulties with grayer aspects of living, such as problem solving, social interactions, and unpredictable circumstances. In different ways, each of the three steps of Plan B can be extremely useful in helping these children handle demands for flexibility and frustration tolerance more adaptively.

The first step—Empathy/Reassurance—is crucial for such children, since they often overreact when faced with the realization that their rigid notions about how events should unfold will not be fulfilled. In many instances, these children are putting rigid solutions on the table rather than concerns, so clarifying their concerns can free up some wiggle room in the solution department. But because the concerns of these children can seem quite unreasonable—even bizarre—to the untrained listener, these children have grown accustomed to having adults (and often peers as well) instantaneously blow their concerns off the table. Rule number one: No matter how bizarre or illogical their concerns may be to you, they're not bizarre or illogical to the child, so it's extremely important to make sure that the child's concerns make it onto the table. This can be very reassuring to a child who's become convinced that his concerns are never taken into account.

The second step of Plan B—Define the Problem—helps the child do something he's never been very good at: taking another person's concerns into account. Once again, the child doesn't have to own your concern to assist in solving the problem, and he doesn't have to care about it; he merely needs to take it into account. Sometimes, helping a rigid, inflexible child simply *hear* someone else's concern without instantaneously exploding is a major achievement.

Finally, the third step of Plan B—the Invitation—helps the child do something else he's never been very good at: adjusting to the idea that there might be some shades of gray somewhere between black and white and that there might be a variety of ways to solve a problem besides the way he originally configured. Early on, this often requires massive doses of reassurance (that the child's concern will be taken into account). And such children often benefit from being reminded about how they have solved similar problems in the past.

Social Skills

In Chapter 3, the different social skills that contribute to a child's capacity for flexibility and frustration tolerance were reviewed, including attending to appropriate social cues and nuances; accurately interpreting those cues; connecting cues with past experience; having a broad repertoire of responses; and recognizing how they're coming across and appreciating how their behavior is affecting others. These skills can take a very long time to learn. Just remember, teaching these skills always takes less time than not teaching them.

We won't cover all of the above skills, but let's sample

a few, starting with accurately interpreting social cues. Some kids trip into some very automatic but inaccurate interpretations of their experiences and the intentions of others, including "It's not fair!," "You always blame me!," "Nobody likes me," and "I'm stupid." These interpretations can cause spontaneous combustion if left unattended.

Adult: Cindy, how do you like school?

Cindy: I hate school.

Adult: You hate school? What is it about school that you hate?

Cindy: I just don't like it.

Adult: That's a shame, because you have to spend a lot of time there. But what is it that you don't like?

Cindy: The other kids think I'm stupid.

Adult: They do? How so?

Cindy: They just do.

Adult: Tell me what you mean by "stupid."

Cindy: You know . . . dumb . . . stupid.

Adult: That must not feel very good to you. What makes you think the other kids think you're stupid? Do they say you're stupid?

Cindy: No, not exactly. I just know they think that.

Adult: Is there anyone else who makes you feel that you're stupid?

Cindy: No.

Adult: Well, there must be some reason you think the other kids think you're stupid. What made you decide that?

Cindy: I sometimes say the wrong answer in class.

Adult: That can be very embarrassing. Can you remember a time when that happened?

Cindy: Well, like last week we were doing math problems on the chalkboard, and my answer was wrong.

Adult: Did the other kids laugh?

Cindy: No, not really.

Adult: Did someone tease you about putting the wrong answer?

Cindy: No.

Adult: Did any of the other kids put the wrong answer?

Cindy: Yes. . . . lots.

Adult: Were they stupid when they put the wrong answer?

Cindy: No.

Adult: What's different when you put the wrong answer?

Cindy: I don't know. I just know they think I'm stupid.

Adult: Hmmm. When you put the wrong answer, you're stupid, but when they put the wrong answer, they're not. I don't get it.

Cindy: Me either.

Adult: It's a little confusing because you get really good grades. How can you be stupid if you get really good grades?

Cindy: I don't know.

Adult: Maybe you're not stupid.

Cindy: No, I'm stupid. Like sometimes I don't understand what I read right away and I have to go back and read it again.

Adult: That happens to me sometimes, too. It's interesting—I don't think I'm stupid because I have to read things twice.

Cindy: That's you.

Adult: Does your teacher know the other kids think you're stupid?

Cindy: Yes.

Adult: What does your teacher say about that?

Cindy: She tells me she thinks I'm very smart.

Adult: Does that help you think you're not stupid?

Cindy: No.

Adult: Is there anything else about school you don't like besides that the other kids think you're stupid?

Cindy: Well, nobody likes me.

Clearly, such inflexible interpretations often defy logic. And in many instances these interpretations contribute to a child's cumulative level of frustration or fuel his frustration at a given moment. In general, when these statements are made only in the context of an explosion, they may simply be a sign that the child is having trouble thinking clearly at that moment. If they occur outside the context of vapor lock and meltdown, the statements may reflect something less fleeting.

Entire books have been written on how to restructure the inaccurate, maladaptive thoughts of children and adults. The idea is to help the individual recognize the inaccuracy of his existing belief systems and replace the inaccurate thoughts that make up these belief systems with a more accurate, adaptive way of thinking. This restructuring usually involves "disconfirming" the individual's old thoughts by presenting—in a user-friendly, low-key, systematic manner—evidence that is contrary to these rigid beliefs. With a child who is stuck on the belief that she's stupid, we might have a teacher or parent whisper the following comment in response to a good grade on an assignment: "I know you sometimes think you're stupid, but I don't think someone who's stupid could have done that well on that math test." In a child who has bona fide weaknesses in one area and strengths in another, a teacher's feedback might be as follows: "I know you're struggling with reading—and that makes you say you're stupid sometimes—but I've never seen anybody who was so good at math. Looks to me like you're really good in math and still need some help in reading." With such feedback being presented continually—not just once or twice—sometimes we can make a dent in a child's inflexible belief system. Parents and teachers do this sort of thing with all children. It just takes on a little more urgency and requires more time, patience, and hard work with explosive children. But it would be a coup for a child who previously summarized her abilities with "I'm stupid" to instead begin saying, "I'm good in math, but I still need help in reading."

Let's think about a few additional social skills. Let's say a child was having difficulty sharing the PlayStation during play-dates. This could reflect difficulty attending to social nuances (for example, that the playmate was pouting or not having a very good time) or difficulty appreciating the impact of one's behavior on others, or both. Let's see what a Proactive Plan B discussion might sound like:

Parent: Jen, was Susie having a good time during your play-date this afternoon?

Jen: I don't know. I guess so.

Parent: I wasn't so sure. I noticed that she didn't look too happy while you were playing with your PlayStation. She was just sitting there.

Jen: She was watching me play.

Parent: I got the impression that maybe she was tired of watching you play and was wishing that she could play, too.

Jen: She didn't say that.

Parent: No . . . but I could tell because her face didn't look very happy.

Jen: Oh.

Parent: You like when Susie comes over to our house, yes?

Jen: Uh-huh.

Parent: Yeah, me too. I'm just a little worried that if she doesn't have a good time she might not want to come over anymore. Yes?

Jen: Yeah.

Parent: So what do you think we should do?

Jen: I could try harder to share with her.

Parent: Yes, you could. That would be great. And I wonder if maybe I could help you notice if Susie's not having such a good time next time she comes over. Just in case you don't notice. What do you think?

Jen: OK.

Proactive B discussions often take much longer than those depicted above, especially on complicated issues like sharing and appreciating how one's behavior is affecting others. And as you now know, the first solution often doesn't get the job done. But at least the concerns are on the table and the ball is now rolling.

9

Family Matters

An explosive child can lay bare many family issues that might never have risen to the surface had the parents been blessed with a less difficult child. But family issues can also complicate or impede implementation of Plan B. Maladaptive family communication patterns, for example, can make it a lot harder for family members to discuss important problems productively; in some instances, these communication patterns can actually fuel explosions. Sibling issues, never easy to deal with under the best circumstances, are even more troublesome when one of the siblings is inflexible, easily frustrated, and explosive. Sometimes parents have difficulties of their own—job stresses, financial problems, or marital issues—that may make it hard to devote extra energy to Plan B. And sometimes grandparents or other relatives don't make the task easier. We'd better take a closer look at these issues.

SIBLINGS

Even in so-called ordinary families, adversarial interactions between siblings can be considered fairly normative. But adding an explosive child to the mix can make standard sibling rivalry look like a walk in the park. For example, though it's not uncommon for "ordinary" siblings to direct their greatest hostility and most savage acts toward each other, these acts can be more intense and traumatizing when they're inflicted—chronically—by an explosive child. And though it's not unusual for "ordinary" siblings to complain about preferential treatment and disparities in parental attention and expectations, these issues can be magnified in families with an explosive child because he may require such a disproportionate share of the parents' resources. Finally, though many siblings seem to get their thrills by antagonizing or teasing one another, an explosive sibling may be considered less capable of responding to such antagonism in an adaptive way; such interactions may therefore have the primary effect of fueling countless explosions.

Fortunately, Plan B can improve interactions among siblings. Depending on their ages, it is often useful to help brothers and sisters understand why their explosive sibling acts the way he does, why his behavior is so difficult to change, how to interact with him in a way that reduces hostility and minimizes the likelihood of aggression or explosions, and what the parents are actively doing to try to improve things. Brothers and sisters tend to be more receptive if there's an improvement in the general tone of family interactions and if the explosive sibling is blowing up less often and becomes an active participant in making things better.

Nonetheless, this understanding doesn't always prevent siblings from complaining about an apparent double standard between themselves and their explosive brother or sister. Armed with the knowledge that parental attention is never distributed with 100 percent parity and parental priorities are never exactly the same for each child in any family, you should resist responding to this complaint by trying even harder to get your explosive child to look like your other children. In all families—yours and everyone else's—*fair does not mean equal.* Even parents in "ordinary" families often find themselves providing one child with more help with homework, having higher academic expectations for one child, or being more nurturing toward another. In your family, you're doing things a little differently for the child who has deficits in the areas of flexibility and frustration tolerance, but you're also doing things differently for the other children, who have challenges of their own. So when siblings are complaining over disparities in parental expectations, it's an excellent opportunity to do some empathizing and educating.

Sister: How come you don't get mad at Danny when he swears at you? It's not fair!

Mother: I know that it's very hard for you to listen to him swearing. I don't like it very much, either. But in our family we try to help one another and make sure everyone gets what he or she needs. I'm trying to help Danny stay calm when he gets frustrated and to help him think of different words he could use instead of swearing. That's what he needs help with.

Sister: But swearing is bad. You should get mad at him when he swears.

Mother: Well, I don't get mad at you when I'm helping you with your math, right? That's because I don't think getting mad at you would help very much. Remember how I used to get mad at Danny whenever he swore? It didn't work very well, did it? It just made things worse. So I'm doing something now that I think will eventually work better. I think it's starting to work pretty well.

Sister: What are you going to do if I start swearing?

Mother: I'd help you think of different words, too. Then again, you don't seem to have a problem with swearing, which is really good. So it doesn't look like that's what you need my help with.

Sister: Yes. Math is what I need help with.

Mother: Exactly.

Can Plan B be applied to interactions between an explosive child and his siblings? Why not? The parents are facilitating Plan B discussions by ensuring that the concerns of both siblings are on the table and that solutions address both concerns. Plan B is still the mechanism by which some essential skills are being taught and problems are being solved, except now in the context of sibling interactions. The brothers and sisters end up feeling good because their explosive sibling is more approachable and less terrifying; they see that their views are being heard, that they are involved in the process of working toward a solution that takes their needs into account, and that you're able to handle things in an evenhanded manner. The explosive child ends up feeling good because you've helped him avoid treating his sibling in a way he'd be sorry for later, helped him work out a solution that takes his needs into account, and reinforced your role as helper. Eventually the goal is for the kids to work out their difficulties without your assistance (which may be occurring some of the time already).

Be forewarned that, in some instances, the behavior of seemingly angelic siblings begins to deteriorate just as the behavior of their explosive brother or sister begins to improve. This is often a sign that the emotional needs of the siblings require closer examination. In some cases, therapy may be necessary for brothers and sisters who have been traumatized by their explosive sibling or who may be manifesting other problems that can be traced back to the old family atmosphere.

If you feel that your family needs help working on these issues, a skilled family therapist can be of great assistance. You may also wish to read an excellent book, *Siblings Without Rivalry* by Adele Faber and Elaine Mazlish.

COMMUNICATION PATTERNS

A family therapist can also help when it comes to making some fundamental changes in how you communicate with your child. Dealing effectively with an explosive child is easier (not easy, *easier*) when patterns of communication between parents and child are adaptive. When these patterns are maladaptive, dealing effectively with such a child is much harder. As you might imagine, some of these patterns are more typical of older explosive kids. But the seeds may be sown early. Although not an exhaustive list, here's a sampling of some of the more common patterns.

Parents and children sometimes get into a vicious cycle—called *speculation*—of drawing erroneous conclusions about each other's motives or cognitions. Others have referred to this pattern as psychologizing or mind reading, and it can sound something like this:

Parent: The reason Oscar doesn't listen to us is that he thinks he's so much smarter than we are.

Now, it's not uncommon for people to make inaccurate inferences about one another. Indeed, responding effectively to these inaccuracies—in other words, setting people straight about yourself in a manner they can understand—is a real talent and requires some pretty complex, rapid processing. Of course, in an explosive child, the demand for complex, rapid processing presents a small problem: he's not very good at it. So while there are some children who can respond to speculation by making appropriate, corrective statements to set the record straight, an explosive child may hear himself being talked about inaccurately and become extremely frustrated. This is an undesirable circumstance in and of itself, but it's especially undesirable because whether Oscar thinks he's smarter than his parents probably isn't worth spending much time discussing. In fact, this topic is a red herring that just distracts everyone from the main issue, which is that Oscar and his parents still haven't figured out how to get past his inflexibility and poor tolerance for frustration so they can discuss and resolve important issues. Of course, speculation can be a two-way street. From a child's mouth, it might sound something like this:

Oscar: The only reason you guys get so mad at me so much is because you like pushing me around.

Such statements can have the same detouring effect, especially when adults follow the careening child in front of them straight through the flashing lights and detour barriers and right off the cliff:

Mother: Yes, that's exactly right, our main goal in life is to push you around. I can't believe you'd say that, after all we've been through with you.

Oscar: Well, what is your main goal then?

Father: Our main goal is to help you be normal.

Oscar: So now I'm not normal. Thank you very much, loser.

Speculation is always going to be a risky undertaking. So how about agreeing on a new family rule: Each family member is allowed to comment only on his or her own thoughts and motivations. In other words, you should speak only for yourself, using "I" statements, such as "I worry about your getting to bed so late" or "I feel very hurt when you say that." If your child does need help articulating his needs or frustrations, your attempts to assist him should be framed tentatively ("Correct me if I'm wrong, but I think what you may be trying to say is . . ." or "Maybe what you're frustrated about is . . .") and should involve an absolute minimum of psychologizing and value judgments. You're also going to need someone to keep conversations on track so they don't swing off the topic. Now, a therapist could be that someone for an hour or two a week. But ultimately, it's going to have to be a family member, and as you may expect, parents are the early frontrunners for this position. Many of the explosions that occur in interactions with explosive children have little to do with the issues that were the main topic of conversation in the first place. When issues are brought up in a way that doesn't elicit defensiveness, most of these children are willing or even eager to talk about important desired topics such as these:

- How they can handle frustration and think things through more adaptively and how you might be able to help.

- How you'd like to start trying to resolve disagreements in a mutually satisfactory manner through civil discussion.

- Things each family member is saying that make another family member defensive and how to communicate with each other in a more productive way.

Of course, it's also critical to listen closely to what the child has to say on these topics; to recognize that it can take the child a long time to spit something out; and to remember that if a child isn't ready to talk about something at a given moment, you probably won't have much luck trying to force the issue. Come back to it later when you've got better odds.

Another maladaptive communication pattern—called *overgeneralization*—refers to the tendency to draw global conclusions in response to isolated events. Here's how it would sound from a parent:

Mother: Billy, maybe you can tell Dr. Collins why you never do your homework.

Billy: What are you talking about?! I do my homework every night!

Mother: Your teachers told me you have a few missing assignments this semester.

Billy: So does everybody! What's the big deal? I miss a few assignments, and you're ready to call in the damn cavalry!

Mother: Why do you always give me such a hard time? I just want what's best for you.

Billy: Stay out of my damn business! That's what's best for me!

What a shame, because there may actually be ways in which Billy's mother could be helpful to him with his homework or at least get some of the reassurance she was looking for about his compliance with homework assignments. Not by starting the discussion with an overgeneralization, though. While other children are sometimes able to get past their parents' overgeneralizations to address the real issues, many explosive children often react strongly to such statements and may lack the skills to respond appropriately with corrective information. Phrasing things tentatively should help you overgeneralize less often ("Oscar, I wonder if we can talk about this without screaming at each other" or "Billy, you'll let me know if there's anything about your homework I can help you with?" or "Myrna, I don't want to bug you about your homework; can we figure out some way for me to know if it's actually getting done?").

In *perfectionism,* parents fail to acknowledge the progress their child has made and demonstrate a tendency to cling to an old, unmodified vision of the child's capabilities. Perfectionism is often driven less by the child's lack of progress and more by the parents' own anxiety. Wherever it's coming from, perfectionism is usually coun-

[illegible]ive with a child who may actually have been [illegible]d to stay on track or who may feel enormously frustra[illegible]d by his parents' unrealistic expectations:

Father: Eric, your mother and I are pretty pleased about how much better you're doing in school, but you're still not working as hard as you ought to be.

Eric: Huh?

Mother: But that's not what we wanted to talk to you about. You're staying up too late doing your homework.

Eric: I get it done, don't I?

Father: Yes, apparently you do, but we want you to get it done earlier so you get more sleep.

Eric: I get enough sleep.

Father: We don't think you do. You're very grouchy in the morning, and you have trouble waking up. We want you to do your homework when you get home from school from now on.

Eric: I'm not doing my homework when I get home from school! I need a break when I get home from school! What difference does it make?

Mother: It makes a difference to us. Now, your father and I have already talked this over, so there's no discussion on it. You need to get your homework done when you get home from school.

Eric: No freaking way.

Hmmm. Eric may or may not actually be interested in thinking about how to get his homework done earlier. Either way, perfectionism (combined with Plan A) is not a particularly effective way to engage him in a discussion on the topic.

Other maladaptive communication patterns include: *sarcasm,* which is either totally lost on explosive children (especially the black-and-white thinking variety) or extremely frustrating to them because they don't have the skills to figure out that the parent meant the exact opposite of what he or she actually said; *put-downs* (Parent: "What's the matter with you?! Why can't you be more like your sister?"); *ruination,* sometimes called "catastrophizing," in which parents greatly exaggerate the effect of current behavior on a child's future well-being (Parent: "We've resigned ourselves to the fact that Hector will probably end up in jail someday"); *interrupting* (Don't forget, the child is probably having trouble sorting through his thoughts in the first place—your interruptions don't help); *lecturing* ("How many times do I have to tell you . . ."); *dwelling on the past* ("Listen, kid, your duck's been upside down in the water for a long time . . . you think I'm gonna get all excited just because you've put together a few good months?"); and *talking through a third person* ("I'm very upset about this, and your father is going to tell you why . . . isn't that right, dear?"). All very counterproductive.

Over time the goal is for you to be able to communicate with your explosive child in a way that demonstrates to him that you can control yourself during discussions, stay on topic, recognize when discussions aren't going anywhere, get the discussion back on track, and deal more adaptively with things that are frustrating to you both. This is very hard to do, and it's made even harder by the fact that you probably have very powerful feelings of your own that influence the way you react to your child. But things can change; you may just need a little help to make them change.

PARENTS

Needless to say, living with an explosive child is a lot easier when adults communicate well enough to implement Plan B. At the least, the adults need to reach a consensus on how they want to approach specific problems or unmet expectations. If you're unable to reach such a consensus, your child will have to continue to handle two completely different sets of expectations, and we already know that boat won't float.

While an explosive child can put pressure on adults' relationships with each other, troubles between a couple can make life with such a child much more difficult to deal with. For partners who aren't even very good at collaboratively solving problems with each other, working things out with a child may be even more challenging.

Partners who are drained by their own difficulties often have little left for a labor-intensive explosive child. Sometimes one partner feels exhausted and resentful about being the primary parent because the other parent spends a lot of time at work. Power struggles that may occur between the adults often affect interactions with the child. And sometimes stepparent issues can enter the mix (Child: "Stay out of this! You're not my real father!" or Stepfather: "That kid was a problem before I arrived on the scene . . . this is between him and his mother"). These issues will need to be addressed, and sometimes marital or family therapy is necessary.

Many parents feel very de-energized by their own personal difficulties. Some parents are quite bitter about having been dealt an explosive hand by the great deck shuffler of children. For one mother, her son's explosions tapped into her own abusive childhood, and it was extremely difficult for her to get past her visceral reaction to her son's raised voice.

Mother: I'm not doing Plan A . . . I'm not going to do to him what my parents did to me.

Therapist: OK.

Mother: But I don't want him walking all over me—that's what my parents did to me—so I'm not doing Plan C.

Therapist: OK.

Mother: So what should I do?

Therapist: Plan B.

Another mother felt so drained by being a full-time parent to her three other children that she simply had no energy left for helping her explosive son. A father had to get a handle on his own explosiveness before he could help his daughter with hers. (He found that many of the Plan B strategies he was using with his daughter helped him explode less often, too.) Another father needed to be medicated for ADHD before he was able to stick to the plan agreed upon in treatment. Yet another father had to come to grips with his excessive drinking and its impact on the whole family before he could press ahead with Plan B. It's hard to work on helping your child if you're feeling the need to put your own house in order first. Take care of yourself. Work hard at creating a support system for yourself. Seek professional help or other forms of support if you need it. These things don't change on their own.

GRANDPARENTS

At times it's necessary to bring grandparents into the therapeutic mix. In many families, grandparents or other relatives function as co-parents, taking care of the children while the parents are at work. We need to make sure the grandparents are "with the program." If grandparents are an integral part of the family unit they need to be brought into the loop. Even if the grandparents don't spend much time with the child—but never miss an opportunity to remind the parents that what the child really needs is a good kick in the pants—they need to be enlightened about why their ideas aren't going to work with their explosive grandchild.

DRAMA IN REAL LIFE

Rules of Communicating

When Mitchell, the fifteen-year-old ninth grader you met in Chapter 3, and his parents arrived for their second session, the therapist was advised that it had been a difficult week.

"We can't talk to him anymore—about anything—without him going crazy," said his mother.

"THAT'S NOT SO, MOTHER!" Mitchell boomed. "I'm not going to sit here and listen to you exaggerate."

"Why don't you stand then?" the father cracked.

Mitchell paused, reflecting on his father's words. "If you were joking, then you're even less funny than I thought you were," he said. "If you weren't, then you're dumber than I thought you were."

"I'm not the one who flunked out of prep school," the father jabbed back.

"AND I'M NOT THE ONE WHO MADE ME GO TO THAT SCHOOL!" Mitchell boomed.

"Look, I'm really not interested in getting into a pissing contest with you, Mitchell," said the father.

"What do you call what you just did?" the mother chimed in. "Anyway, I don't think Mitchell is ready to face flunking out of prep school yet."

"DON'T SPEAK FOR ME, MOTHER!" Mitchell boomed. "YOU DON'T KNOW WHAT I'M READY TO FACE!"

"Pardon me for interrupting," the therapist said, "but is this the way conversations usually go in this family?"

"Why? Do you think we're all lunatics?" asked Mitchell.

"Speak for yourself," said the father.

"Screw you," said Mitchell.

"Well, we're off to a wonderful start, aren't we?" said the mother.

"WE ARE NOT OFF TO A WONDERFUL START, MOTHER!" Mitchell boomed.

"I was being sarcastic," said the mother. "I thought a little humor might lighten things up a bit."

"I'm not amused," Mitchell grumbled.

"Fortunately, we're not here to amuse you," said the father.

"Sorry to interrupt you folks again," the therapist

said. "But I'm still wondering if this is a pretty typical conversation."

"Oh, Mitchell would have gotten insulted and stormed out of the room if we were at home," said the mother. "In fact, I'm surprised he's still sitting here now."

"YOU HAVE NO IDEA HOW I FEEL!" boomed Mitchell.

"We've been listening to you telling us how you feel since you were a baby," said the father. "We know more about how you feel than you know."

"ENOUGH!" boomed Mitchell.

"My sentiments exactly," the therapist said. "I think I'll answer my own question. Forgive me for being so direct, but you guys have some not-so-wonderful ways of communicating with one another."

"How do you mean?" asked the mother.

"You're a very sarcastic group," the therapist said. "Which would be fine, I guess, except that when you're sarcastic, I think it makes it very hard for Mitchell to figure out what you mean."

"But he's so smart and we're so dumb," said the father.

Mitchell paused, reflecting on his father's words. "Are you trying to be funny again?" he asked his father.

"You're so smart, figure it out," the father said.

"Uhm," the therapist interrupted, "I'm sure you guys could do this all day, but I don't think it would get us anywhere."

Mitchell chuckled. "He still thinks we're going to accomplish something by coming here," he said into the air.

"I should add that sarcasm isn't the only bad habit," the therapist continued. "The one-upmanship in this family is intense."

"Birds of a feather," the mother chirped.

"What does that mean?" Mitchell demanded.

"It means that the apple didn't fall far from the tree," said the mother.

"Be careful about whose tree you're talking about," said the father. "I don't want any credit for this."

"Oh, I'm afraid you're right in the thick of things," the therapist reassured the father. "I wonder if we could establish a few rules of communicating. I must warn you, I'm not sure you'll have much to say to one another once I tell you these rules."

"Bravo," said Mitchell. "That's music to my ears."

"What kind of rules?" asked the mother.

"Well, it would be a lot more productive if we got rid of a lot of the sarcasm," the therapist said. "It really muddies up the communication waters. And the one-upmanship has got to go."

The ensuing silence was broken by the father. "I don't think he can do it," he said, looking at Mitchell.

Before Mitchell could erupt, the therapist interjected, "That's one-upmanship."

Mitchell's frown turned upside down. "Thank you," he said.

"This is going to be hard," said the father. "And no more sarcasm either?"

"Not if you guys want your son to start talking to you again," the therapist said.

"Where's that team spirit, fellas?" the mother chimed in.

"That's sarcasm," the therapist interjected.

"Ooo, this guy is tough," said the father, turning to his wife. "I don't like coming here anymore." He smiled.

"That's sarcasm, too," the therapist said.

"My husband isn't accustomed to being corrected," said the mother.

"Oh, that reminds me of the last bad habit," the therapist said.

"Oh, God, what did I say?" the mother said, covering her mouth.

"You guys talk for one another a lot," the therapist said, "like you can read one another's minds."

"Well, we know one another very well," said the mother.

"That may be," the therapist said, "but from what I've observed, your speculations about one another are often off-target, and they don't go over very well."

"What'd you call it?" asked the mother.

"Speculation," the therapist said. "Thinking you

know what's going on in someone's head. It just gets you guys more agitated with one another."

"No more speculation?" said the mother.

"Not if you guys want to actually start talking to one another," the therapist confirmed.

"What should we do if someone does one of those three things?" Mitchell asked.

"Just point it out to them without being judgmental," the therapist said. "If someone is sarcastic, just say, 'That's sarcasm.' If someone is one-upping, say, 'That's one-upmanship.' And if someone is speculating, say . . ."

" 'That's speculation,' " said Mitchell.

"My, we catch on fast," said the father.

"That's sarcasm," said Mitchell.

Does the CPS model ever fail to work? What then?

There's good reason to be optimistic that, with your help, your explosive child will be able to respond to frustration more adaptively. These are resilient kids—they do respond to being understood and to good treatment.

Most of the time. There are, unfortunately, children who do not have access to, refuse to participate in, or do not respond as favorably to treatment and who continue to behave in an unsafe manner at home, at school, and/or in the community. Many started a downward spiral early, became increasingly alienated, began exhibiting more serious forms of inappropriate behavior, and began to hang out with other children who have come down a similar path.

Unfortunately, society isn't yet well prepared to help these children. Many school personnel don't have the experience or expertise to handle the difficulties of students whose learning disability is in the domains of flexibility and frustration tolerance. Many alternative day-school placements still use traditional reward and punishment programs as their primary therapeutic modality. The police and courts often aren't equipped to provide the type of intervention needed by many families. Often, the best the judicial system can do is hold the threat of a significant consequence over a child's head. Many social service agencies are overwhelmed; the problems of an explosive child and his family may pale in comparison to the problems of other children and families that are referred to and followed by these agencies. Mental health professionals aren't especially effective in working with individuals who won't come in for treatment or whose needs require attention outside the boundaries of a fifty-minute session in a therapist's office. And managed care issues are sometimes a significant obstacle.

After all else has been tried—therapy, medication, perhaps even alternative day-school placements—what many of these children ultimately need is a change of environment. A new start. A way to start working on a new identity. Once alienation and deviance become a child's identity and a means of being a part of something, things are a lot harder to turn around. Many such children ultimately need treatment that is more intensive than the kind that can be provided on an outpatient basis or in a regular education setting. One way to give them this new start is by placing them in a therapeutic facility. As horrible as that may sound, there are some outstanding residential facilities in the United States that do an exceptional job of working with such children.

The better residential facilities have excellent academic programs, so a child's chance of being accepted to college isn't sacrificed. Although many of these facilities have a behavior management component for maintaining order, the better ones also have a strong therapeutic component through which many of the thinking and communicating skills described in the preceding chapters can be developed. Many of them also have a family therapy component (remember, the goal is for the child to return to his own home and community). Residential programs whose primary agents of change are large human beings who make sure your child knows who's boss should be avoided.

The prospect of placing one's child in a residential facility can feel like a nightmare to many parents, although parents who have been living a constant nightmare at home are often more open to the idea. Our instincts are to keep our families together, even when they're being torn apart. Our instincts are to keep our children under our supervision, even when our supervision is no longer sufficient. We don't like to feel that we're throwing in the towel, even when all the evidence suggests we cannot provide everything a child needs. We don't like asking someone else to take care of our child, even when we think it may be for the best. So our every instinct is to hang on, tough it out, and try something else. A new drug. A new therapist. A new program. A new school. A new book.

If a child is acting out in school, it is sometimes possible to convince or compel a school system to pay for a placement outside the school system. Under the Individuals with Disabilities Act (a federal law, and it's a good one, that applies to public schools), school systems are obliged to place their students in the least restrictive setting appropriate to their needs; residential placements are considered the most restrictive setting, so such placements are generally held out as a last resort. School systems vary widely in their resources for children who need more than the mainstream can provide. If it becomes apparent, after adjustments and accommodations are made, that a general education program is not sufficient for your child's needs, the first consideration in many school systems is a classroom aide. The next stop is often a special classroom for children with behavioral problems. A day-school placement outside the school system is frequently the next stop. If these alternatives fail to achieve the desired effect, a residential program may become a more serious consideration. In some cases, if it's clear that these intermediate placements are insufficient for a child's needs, a residential program may be considered earlier in the process.

If you end up seriously considering placing your child in a residential facility, try to visit some of the places where you're thinking of sending him. Make sure you feel comfortable with the staff, the philosophy of the program, and the other children at the facility. Make sure the staff have lots of experience working with children whose profiles are similar to your child's. Make sure they are open to your ideas about your child.

Placement won't be forever. With luck, only a year or two. That gives you some time to get your own house in order, while your child is in a controlled, safe environment where he can learn how to think more flexibly and handle frustration more adaptively, where he can get his medication straight, and where he can be helped to come home. It's not the end of the world. It can be a new beginning.

10

Better Living Through Chemicals

As noted in Chapter 7, there are some children who will not benefit substantially from the approach described in this book until they've been satisfactorily medicated. No one wants to see a child medicated unnecessarily, so a conservative approach to medication is recommended. However, some characteristics are well addressed by medication; namely, hyperactivity and poor impulse control, inattention and distractibility, irritability and obsessiveness, and having an exceedingly short fuse. Medication does not teach a child thinking skills, but when it's effective, it can open the door to such teaching. The goal of this chapter is to provide a brief overview of (rather than a comprehensive guide to) the medical options.

Deciding whether to medicate one's child should be difficult; you'll need a lot of information, much more than is provided in this chapter. Ultimately, what you'll need most of all is an outstanding child psychiatrist. You'll want one who

- takes the time to get to know you and your child, listens to you, and is familiar with treatment options that have nothing to do with a prescription pad

- knows that a diagnosis provides little useful information about your child

- understands that there are many things medication doesn't treat well at all

- has a good working knowledge of the potential side effects of medication and their management

- makes sure that you—and your child, if it's appropriate—understand each medication and its anticipated benefits and potential side effects and interactions with other medications

- is willing to devote sufficient time to monitoring your child's progress carefully and continually over time

- continually evaluates when it's time to consider taking your child off his medication

When children have a poor response to medication, it is often because one of the foregoing elements was missing from their treatment.

All medications—aspirin included—have side effects. Your doctor should help you weigh the anticipated benefits of medication against the potential risks so that you can make educated decisions. Although it's important to have faith in the doctor's expertise, it's equally important that you feel comfortable with the treatment plan he or she proposes, or at least that you're comfortable with the balance between benefits and risks. If you are not comfortable with or confident in the information you've been given, you need more information. If your doctor doesn't have the time or expertise to provide you with more information, you need a new doctor. Medical treatment is not something to fear, but it needs to be implemented and monitored competently and compassionately.

Not all the medications described here have been officially approved for use with kids, and many have not been studied extensively in use with children and adolescents, especially with regard to their long-term side effects.

INATTENTION AND DISTRACTIBILITY

If inattention and distractibility are significantly interfering with your child's academic progress or with his ability to participate in Plan B discussions, medication may offer some promise. The mainstays of medical treatment for inattention and cognitive inefficiency are the stimulant medications, some of which have been in use for more than sixty years. This category of medicines include well known, well studied agents such as methylphenidate (Ritalin) and dextroamphetamine sulfate (Dexedrine). Stimulants come in short- and long-acting preparations. In most cases, the side effects associated with stimulants tend to be mild, but they are worth mentioning. Two of the more common side effects are insomnia (especially if a full dose is administered after the mid- to late-afternoon hours) and loss of appetite, which can, over the long term, result in weight loss. In some children, stimulants may unmask or exacerbate existing vocal or motor tics (this circumstance may require adding a second medication to reduce the tics or discontinuing the stimulant medication). Stimulants may increase anxiety and irritability in some children, an undesirable circumstance for any child but perhaps especially an explosive one. The behavior of some children can deteriorate when stimulant medication wears off (a phenomenon called rebound), and this side effect is sometimes addressed by administering a half dose late in the afternoon to ease the child off the medication. Finally, particularly in adolescents, parents need to be aware of the potential for abusing stimulants.

HYPERACTIVITY AND POOR IMPULSE CONTROL

If hyperactivity and poor impulse control are significantly interfering with your child's behavior at home or at school or his academic progress, or with his ability to participate in Plan B discussions, medication may help. Several classes of medications can be helpful, and stimulants are, again, often the agents of first choice. However, in some children, side effects, the lack of a positive response to stimulants, or complicating conditions may require consideration of alternative medications for enhancing impulse control and reducing hyperactivity, such as a relatively new nonstimulant medication called atomoxetine (Strattera). Side effects of this medication include upset stomach, decreased appetite, nausea or vomiting, dizziness, fatigue, and mood swings.

An atypical antidepressant called bupropion (Wellbutrin) has also been used to ameliorate hyperactivity-impulsivity in children. Bupropion may increase the risk of seizures; exacerbate tics; cause insomnia, nausea, headache, constipation, tremor, and dry mouth; and can initially cause an increase in agitation. Antihypertensive medications, including clonidine (Catapres) and guanfacine (Tenex) are also sometimes used to reduce hyperactivity and impulsivity, but they may be less effective for inattention. Antihypertensives can also be effective at reducing tics. In addition, because of their sedating effect, antihypertensives have been used to help children sleep at night. However, in some children, this sedation may be a problem during daytime hours and is sometimes manifested in the form of heightened irritability. In those explosive children whose difficulties involve the emotion regulation pathway, increased irritability is undesirable. Side effects can include headache, dizziness, nausea, constipation, and dry mouth.

The tricyclic antidepressants, which include agents such as nortriptyline (Pamelor), desipramine (Norpramin), imipramine (Tofranil), and clomipramine (Anafranil), may also be prescribed to reduce hyperactivity and impulsiveness in children. An advantage of tricyclic medications is that they provide twenty-four-hour coverage and typically do not interfere with sleep. One of the rare but more serious side effects of the tricyclic medications is cardiac toxicity, which often necessitates that children medicated with such agents undergo initial and then periodic electrocardiograms. There are a variety of additional potential side effects that may not be well tolerated by children, including dry mouth, weight gain, sedation, lightheadedness, and constipation.

IRRITABILITY AND OBSESSIVENESS

If irritability or obsessiveness is significantly interfering with your child's functioning at home or school, or with his ability to participate in Plan B discussions, medication may help. Irritability and obsessiveness in children have most often been treated with a group of medications called selective serotonin re-uptake inhibitors (SSRI anti-depressants), which include agents such as fluoxetine (Prozac), sertraline (Zoloft), paroxetine (Paxil), citalopram (Celexa), and fluvoxamine (Luvox). However, as of this writing, the use of these medications has become controversial owing to findings that these agents can cause increased suicidal thinking in some children (a fact that some of the manufacturers of these agents were apparently not completely forthcoming in disclosing). Other side effects include nausea, weight loss or weight gain, anxiety, nervousness, insomnia, and sweating.

EXTREMELY SHORT FUSE

If—despite heavy doses of Plan C—your child's fuse is still so short that he is incapable of participating in Plan B discussions, a class of medications called atypical antipsychotics—including medications such as risperidone (Risperdal), olanzipine (Zyprexa), quetiapine (Seroquel), and aripiprazole (Abilify) may be used. These medications have prompted much enthusiasm because they tend to be better tolerated than more traditional antipsychotics. However, these agents have been associated with sedation and significant weight gain, and may be associated with extrapyramidal symptoms, such as odd mouth or tongue movements, eye rolling, rigidity in the limbs, fixed facial expression, blank emotions, and involuntary movements. These symptoms typically subside once the medication is discontinued; however, in rare instances, they may persist even after the child is taken off the medication (a condition called tardive dyskinesia).

Another class of agents—broadly referred to as mood stabilizers—may also be prescribed, including lithium carbonate, carbamazepine (Tegretol), and valproic acid (Depakote). The mood stabilizers may be less effective in children who are predominantly dysphoric. Indeed, because these agents may produce drowsiness or fatigue, they may actually increase irritability in some children. All of these agents provide twenty-four-hour coverage and typically do not affect the sleep of most children. Lithium can cause sedation, nausea, diarrhea, thirst, increased urination, mild tremor, and weight gain, and must be monitored closely. Valproic acid and carbamazepine may cause sedation, nausea, diarrhea, heartburn, tremor, and weight gain. Valproic acid can also cause liver toxicity, and carbamazepine can be associated with a decrease in white blood cell count and aplastic anemia, so the use of these agents requires periodic bloodwork.

Less traditional agents such as flaxseed oil and fish oil have also been shown to have promising mood stabilizing effects. Indeed, some children may benefit from nontraditional, natural, or homeopathic agents. Although it's fine to be open to the use of such agents, it's important to note that they do have a chemical effect on a child's body (we have a tendency to view "natural" agents as somehow more benign), can produce undesirable side effects, often have not been carefully studied (of course, the same can be said about many of the traditional psychiatric medications presently being prescribed for children), and must be taken under the supervision of a qualified professional.

At the risk of redundancy, it should be clear that the most crucial component in the psychopharmacology picture is a competent, clinically savvy, attentive, available prescribing doctor. But the doctor can't treat your child successfully unless he or she receives accurate information from you and your child's teachers about the effects of the prescribed medications. When all relevant adults work in concert with the doctor, side effects are handled more efficiently and adjustments are made more responsively. A discreet approach to medication is also recommended. Most children aren't eager for their classmates to know that they're receiving medication for emotional or behavioral purposes. And there's a temptation for parents to keep school personnel in the dark about their child's medication status as well. True to the collaborative spirit required for intervening effectively with explosive children, and because the observations and feedback of teachers are often crucial to making appropriate adjustments in medication, I generally encourage parents to keep relevant school personnel in the loop on medications. If there's no way to keep a child's classmates in the dark, it's often necessary to educate the classmates about individual differences (asthma, allergies, diabetes, difficulty concentrating, low frustration tolerance, and the like) that may require medicinal treatment.

If you choose to medicate your child, for how long will you have to use medication? That's hard to predict. In general, the chemical benefits of these agents endure only as long as the medication is taken. Nonetheless, in some children, the behavioral improvements that are facilitated by medication persist even after the medications are discontinued, especially if a child has acquired new compensatory skills. Ultimately, the question of whether a child should remain on medication must be continuously revisited.

11

The Plan B Classroom

As hard as it is to help an explosive child within a family, it may be even harder in a classroom in the company of an additional twenty-five to thirty kids, many of whom have other types of special needs themselves. Like parents, most general education teachers have never been responsible for helping an explosive child and have never received any specialized training to prepare them for this task.

Fortunately, most explosive kids don't actually show any signs of explosiveness at school. Here are a few possible explanations for this phenomenon, including some mentioned earlier:

- *The embarrassment factor*: They'd be embarrassed if they exploded in front of their peers. Since the embarrassment factor can't be replicated at home, embarrassment doesn't prevent the child from blowing up at home.

- *The tightly wrapped factor*: The child has put so much energy into holding it together at school that he becomes unraveled the minute he gets home, fueled further by normal late-afternoon fatigue and hunger.

- *The herd-mentality factor*: Because the school day tends to be relatively structured and predictable, it can actually be user-friendlier than unstructured downtime at home. For instance, if a child becomes confused about where he's supposed to be or what he's supposed to be doing while he's at school, he need look no further than his classmates for cues. The herd-mentality factor can't be replicated at home either.

- *The chemical factor*: Teachers and peers often are the primary beneficiaries of pharmacotherapy, but the medications may have worn off by late afternoon or early evening.

There are probably other possibilities. But just because a child isn't exploding at school doesn't mean that school isn't contributing to explosions that occur elsewhere. Lots of things can happen at school to fuel explosions outside of school: being teased by other children, feeling socially isolated or rejected, feeling frustrated and embarrassed over struggles on certain academic tasks, being misunderstood by the teacher. And homework can extend school frustrations well after the bell rings at the end of the school day. So schools aren't off the hook for helping, even if they don't see the child at his worst.

Of course, there are lots of kids who do explode at school. You may recall that Casey, one of the children you read about in Chapter 4, had a pattern of running out of the classroom when he became frustrated by a challenging academic task or difficult interaction with a peer. When he wasn't running out of the room, he was exploding in the room, turning red, crying, screaming, crumpling paper, breaking pencils, falling on the floor, and refusing to work. Danny, another of the children you read about in Chapter 4, was also capable of the occasional explosion at school. On one particularly memorable day, the teacher designated him to hand out doughnuts to his classmates after recess. Following recess, he hurried back to the classroom to hand out the doughnuts, but a parent-aide was already in the room and insisted on being the doughnut distributor. Danny attempted to explain to the parent that he had been assigned the task of giving out the doughnuts, but the parent would not be deterred. The shift in cognitive set demanded by this example of reciprocal inflexibility was more than Danny could handle. *Kaboom.*

Teachers and schools have little choice but to put some serious thought into how to handle the Caseys and Dannys in their midst. We live in the era of inclusion (by the way, that's a good thing), which has encouraged including students with special behavioral and academic needs in mainstream classrooms, thereby providing these students with opportunities to interact with "ordinary" kids (and vice versa) and reducing the stigma of having special needs addressed outside of the classroom. Thus, a typical mainstream classroom is now likely to have numerous special needs students, some of whom have disorders their teachers have never even heard of, let alone worked with, before. Teachers must therefore have expertise not only in the curriculum but also in the different emotional and behavioral issues presented by some of their students and how to handle those issues effectively. Unfortunately, in many instances teachers feel—justifiably—that they have not had the training and are not being provided with the kind of support they need to function effectively with students with emotional and behavioral challenges.

To make things worse, in the United States we also live in the era of high-stakes testing, which places expectations on teachers to try to ensure that every square peg fits into the round holes defined by the standards imposed by statewide mandated testing. Not even a good idea if you're interested in raising standards, but most assuredly not a good idea if you want teachers to respond to the behavioral, social, and learning needs of individual students.

And to make things still worse, the zero-tolerance driven discipline program in most schools is very much a road map for Plan A: It's a list (sometimes a very long one) of things students can and can't do and a list (sometimes a very long one) of what's going to happen if they do or don't do those things. But here's a true fact you might want to ponder for a moment: Standard school disciplinary practices don't work for the students to whom they are most frequently applied, and aren't needed for the students to whom they are never applied. In other words, the school discipline program isn't the reason well-behaved students behave well; they behave well because they *can*. We have little to show for all the consequences—detentions, suspensions, expulsions, and so forth—that are meted out on a daily basis to the explosive students in our midst. And yet the standard rationale for the continued use of consequences goes something like this:

Administrator: We have to set an example for all our students; even if suspension doesn't help Rickey, at least it sets an example for our other students. We need to let them know that we take safety seriously at our school.

Question: What message do you give the other students at your school if you continue to apply interventions that aren't helping Rickey behave more adaptively?

Answer: That you're actually not sure how to help Rickey behave more adaptively.

Question: What's the likelihood that the students who aren't explosive would become explosive if you did not make an example of Rickey?

Answer: As a general rule, slim to none.

Question: What message do we give Rickey if we continue to apply strategies that aren't working?

Answer: We don't understand you and we can't help you.

Question: Under what circumstances do we have the best chance of helping Rickey learn and practice better ways of dealing with his inflexibility and low frustration tolerance: in school or suspended from school?

Answer: In school.

Question: Why do many schools continue to use interventions that aren't working for their explosive students?

Answer: They aren't sure what else to do.

Question: What happens to students to whom these interventions are counterproductively applied for many years?

Answer: They become more alienated and fall further outside the social fabric of the school.

Question: Isn't this the parents' job?

Answer: Helping a child deal more adaptively with frustration is everyone's job. Besides, the parents aren't there when the child's exploding at school.

Question: Isn't this the job of special education?

Answer: No, special education really has very little to offer many explosive students.

Time for Plan B. But let's make sure the wagon is packed before we start heading into the wilderness. We're going to need a few things:

- *A Philosophy:* Most schools don't have a philosophy about children. What they have instead is a curriculum and a school discipline code, neither of which is of much use when trying to figure out why a student is exploding and how to teach him the skills he needs to stop exploding. Your philosophy about children is what guides and governs your response when a student is not doing well. What's your new philosophy? You might want to consider *children do well if they can*. That way you won't waste a lot of time trying to "teach him a lesson" or find ways to give a student the incentive to do well. Good teachers know that although it would be more efficient to have all the students in a classroom have the exact same learning styles and capabilities, it never works out that way. So it's always necessary to adapt lessons and assignments to individual learners. The learning disability of inflexibility and poor tolerance for frustration is as good a reason to do Plan B as any other type of learning disability.

- *Time:* Teachers often complain that they don't have time to do Plan B. Of course, doing the right thing and fixing the problem always takes less time than doing the wrong thing and not fixing the problem. But it's absolutely true that the school schedule isn't designed to give school personnel the time they need to discuss a student's pathways, develop action plans for teaching the thinking skills a child lacks and using Plan B, and meeting periodically to assess the student's progress and reconfigure the action plan. On the other hand, what's done with the meeting time that does exist is often—don't take this the wrong way, please—a waste of time. Too much time is spent telling stories (about the student's behavior) rather than making sense out of the stories with the pathways. Too much time is spent agonizing and obsessing over categorization ("Does he need a 504 Plan or an IEP?") rather than developing action plans to get the job done.

- *Expertise:* Many educators apply to explosive students the same principles of discipline that were effective with their own children, generally with poor results. Other educators believe that the expertise necessary for understanding and helping an explosive child is well beyond their grasp. Not true. You need expertise in three domains: *five pathways, three Plans, and three steps for doing Plan B.* So chin up: If you've read the ten chapters that preceded this one, you're well on your way in the expertise department. Now you just need experience. No time like the present.

- *A Plan B Road Map:* We're going to have to replace the school discipline code with something that will actually work: a road map for implementing Plan B. It's a pretty easy road map to follow. The first goal is to achieve a consensus on a given student's pathways and triggers (see Chapter 3). This usually requires a meeting or two involving all of the adults who interact with the child at school. It often makes sense to have parents and relevant mental health professionals present as well. Intervening before you know what pathways and triggers are coming into play is akin to a hunter firing a shotgun randomly into the air and hoping to hit something good. The next goal is to prioritize which problems are to be proactively solved (triggers) and which skills are to be proactively taught (pathways), then to determine the specific roles each adult is to play in helping with the Plan B problem solving and teaching. Even if the initial action plan goes well, the whole crew should reconvene periodically to gauge progress, revisit triggers and pathways, adjust goals, and revise the action plan accordingly.

In creating the action plan, it's important to bear in mind some of the principles discussed in earlier chapters. First, *there is no quick fix*. It's worth repeating: You don't fix a reading disability in a week, and you don't fix this learning disability in a week either. Second, *ensuring good communication among adults is absolutely essential*. All the adults who interact with the child must have a clear understanding of his unique difficulties, the skills to implement Plan B, and knowledge of the action plan. Third, *blaming doesn't help*. When things are going poorly at school, parents have a tendency to blame the school staff, and school personnel have a tendency to blame the parents. Blaming misses the important point: The child is frustrating all of us, and none of us has done an incredible job of helping him yet, so let's see if we can put our heads together and come up with a plan that incorporates the best we all have to offer.

Let's apply the above Plan B principles to a very common trigger, homework, which may well be the most common cause of explosions. Many explosive children find homework to be extremely frustrating, perhaps because they don't have any brain energy left after a long day at school, or because their medication has worn off, or because they have learning problems that make homework completion an agonizing task, or because homework—especially long-term assignments—requires a lot of organization and planning. Thus, it's no accident that these children often exhibit some of their most extreme explosiveness while they're trying to do homework. Do these difficulties render some children incapable of completing the same homework assignments as their classmates? Sometimes. Does having a child explode routinely over homework help him feel more successful about, and set the stage for, future completion of homework? No. With Plan A, the teacher is simply insisting that a child complete his homework, regardless of the toll it takes on the child and on the folks who are enforcing the teacher's will at home. With Plan C, the teacher is dropping the homework expectation completely.

And with Plan B? First, we're going to operate on the assumption that if the student could do all the homework you've assigned, he would. Then we're going to get a good handle on the factors (including pathways) that are contributing to the child's difficulties on homework. Then we're going to apply the expertise we've obtained from the preceding chapters and engage the child and/or his parent(s) in a Plan B discussion. Here's how it might sound with a parent:

Teacher (Empathy, Proactive Plan B): Ms. May, I understand that homework has been very difficult lately.

Mother: Homework has been very difficult for a very long time. You're the first teacher Jimmy's had who's expressed any interest in what we go through with homework. We spend several hours fighting over homework every weeknight.

Teacher: I'm sorry about that. But let's see if we can come up with a plan so it's not so terrible anymore.

Mother: You can't imagine how nice that would be.

Teacher: Now, I know Jimmy has a lot of trouble with writing. Safe to assume that's part of the problem with homework?

Mother: Writing's a problem . . . and there are some assignments that he just doesn't seem to understand at all.

Teacher: Can you give me a sense about which assignments seem to be hard for him to understand?

Mother: Science. Definitely science. Sometimes social studies. Math he gets done in about ten minutes.

Teacher (clarifying Empathy): Yes, we've noticed math seems to be his thing. But we've got writing troubles and problems with science and social studies. Interesting, those are the subjects that also require the most writing. Do you think it's the writing or the material?

Mother: I think it's both.

Teacher: Well, let's take our problems one at a time. Let's start with the easier one. I've read Jimmy's IEP, and of course I've had him in my class for about six weeks now, but I can't say I have a perfect handle on which parts of science and social studies are hard for him yet. So I'm thinking you can help me figure it out. I'm thinking that, for the time being, if he's having trouble with a science or social studies homework assignment, you stop doing the assignment and write me a note letting me know what part seemed to be hard. Then I can get a sense about what's getting in his way. Then we'll figure out what to do next. Sound OK to you?

Mother: It sounds OK to me, except for one part. Sometimes he's the one who's insisting on getting it done! He doesn't want to be different, and he's afraid you'll be mad.

Teacher: I'll talk with him about that so he'll know I'm on board with the plan. Let's think about the other problem. I don't want to give up on Jimmy and writing. I know it's hard for him, and we're doing the keyboarding at school, but I don't want him to think he never has to write.

Mother: I agree.

Teacher: OK, let's put our heads together and think about what we can do about this. I'm wondering if we should have Jimmy be part of the discussion so we're sure we've got a solution that everyone's OK with. What do you think?

Mother: Sounds good to me.

What's the solution to the writing problem? There are dozens of possibilities. The most important thing to remember is that durable solutions are those that are realistic, doable, and mutually satisfactory. And that sometimes the problem doesn't get solved with the first solution.

Emergency Plan B is an option as well, but one you don't want to rely on too often:

Rickey (age thirteen): I'm not working on this assignment right now.

Teacher: Well, then your grade will reflect both your attitude and your lack of effort.

Rickey: I don't give a damn about my grades, man. I can't do this crap.

Teacher: Your mouth just got you a detention, young man. And I don't want students in my classroom who don't do their work. Anything else you'd like to say?

Rickey: Yeah . . . This class sucks.

Teacher: Nor do I need to listen to this. You need to go to the assistant principal's office . . . now.

Oops. That was Plan A, wasn't it? Tricky author. Let's see what it would really have looked like with Emergency Plan B:

Rickey: I'm not working on this assignment right now.

Teacher: Is there something about the assignment that's hard for you? Let's see if we can figure it out.

Rickey: Forget it . . . I can't do this! Just leave me alone! Damn!

Teacher: Rickey, listen a second. I know you have trouble with writing and spelling, and you get very frustrated when you have to do assignments where you have to write and spell. Let's see if we can find a way for you to do the important part of the assignment—letting me know what you thought of the story you just heard, which is something you're very good at—without you getting all frustrated about the writing and spelling part.

Rickey: How?

Teacher: Well, maybe Darren would help you write down your thoughts. You could sort of dictate your thoughts to him.

Rickey: It's not worth it. No way.

Teacher: Oh yeah . . . I sometimes forget you're embarrassed about how you spell. Why don't we have you and Darren do the assignment as a team and just make sure he does the writing part?

Rickey: You won't tell him I can't spell?

Teacher: Not if you don't want me to.

Rickey: Darren, let's do this thing together!

Much better. You don't mind a little feedback, right? Rickey's writing and spelling problems are *predictable*. Let's get that problem solved by doing Proactive Plan B . . . soon!

Of course, doing Plan B with an individual student is a whole lot easier if you're doing Plan B with your entire classroom. In other words, there's no down side to using Plan B with all your students.

It'll be a whole lot easier if you put some energy into *creating a community of learners*. How do you do that? First, by emphasizing a social curriculum as much as you do the academic curriculum. Another curriculum?! Don't put the book down just yet. Teachers who put a lot of energy into a social curriculum find that the community of learners they've created actually facilitates the academic curriculum they need to teach. So we're talking about planned and unplanned group discussions on hearing one another's concerns, generating alternative solutions, coming to mutually satisfactory outcomes. Yes, it makes sense to interrupt other ongoing lessons to process important social issues that have suddenly erupted in the classroom. All students benefit from such discussions but especially those who need it most. The teacher acts as a role model and provides frequent opportunities for practicing social interactions and helping one another, including peer tutoring, judicious seating arrangements, and cooperative learning. Still reading? Good.

Your social curriculum also helps you celebrate and accentuate individual differences. Everyone in the classroom has strengths that can be used to help other students, and everyone has areas of weakness in which they need help. This isn't a tit-for-tat classroom . . . in your classroom, everyone gets what he or she needs. Indeed, because of the emphasis on individual differences, students are taught that your expectation is that they will help one another. They learn that each classmate is an integral thread in the fabric of a community of learners. Each student is working on something with Plan B. Rather than being overwhelmed, the teacher has a sense about the unique emotional, social, and behavioral needs of each student and a framework for trying to meet those needs within the context of the larger group.

In one first-grade classroom, a visitor was observing one day and noticed one child (it turns out he was the explosive one) helping another student with her math (it turns out the helper was quite skilled in math and the helpee was not). Several minutes later, when it was time to switch activities (from math to music), the math whiz became stuck. The girl he'd been helping with math calmed him down, talked to him, and helped him move on to music (turns out she was very good at dealing with frustration), all within eyeshot of the teacher. Then the girl, apparently recognizing that the visitor might not have comprehended what was going on, came over and softly explained, "He just gets a little frustrated sometimes." A lot of teachers who wish they could be helpful to the explosive student in their classroom—but feel they don't have sufficient time to devote to him—simply need to be made aware of the help available from the most probable and willing candidates—the other kids.

Teacher: "I can't have different sets of rules for different kids. If I let one child get out of or get away with something, my other students will want to as well."

First of all, you probably have different expectations for different children already, so in classrooms, as in families, *fair does not mean equal* anyway. That's why some students are receiving special reading help while others are not; why some students are in a gifted program for math while others are not. If a student asks why one of his classmates is being treated differently, you have the perfect opportunity to do some educating: "Everyone in our classroom gets what he or she needs. If someone needs help with something, we all try to help him or her. And everyone in our class needs something special." It's no different when a child needs help with flexibility and frustration tolerance. So our response to the student who asks why an explosive classmate is receiving some sort of special accommodations and assistance would sound very similar: "Everyone in our classroom gets what he or she needs. If someone needs help with something, we all try to help him or her. Because you're very good at handling frustration, I bet you could be very helpful to Johnny the next time he gets frustrated."

Do you really think that a child who typically behaves appropriately will decide to behave inappropriately because accommodations are being made for an explosive child in the classroom? Sounds pretty far-fetched. It follows that punishing a child to set an example for or to be fair to the others—especially when there's no expectation that the punishment will be an effective intervention for the child being punished—makes little sense. In a community of learners, the academic or behavioral idiosyncrasies of one student are an opportunity for his or her classmates to help and learn, not to follow suit. The other students are waiting to see if you know what you're doing, not to see whether you're good at treating everybody exactly the same. And since everyone's different, why would the goal ever be to treat everyone exactly the same?

Children are actually pretty good at understanding the fair-does-not-mean-equal concept and at making exceptions for children who need help; in my experience, it's much more common that adults are the ones struggling with the principle.

DRAMA IN REAL LIFE

Running on Empty

"We can't let Casey keep running out of the room," the school principal said gravely. "It's dangerous, and we're responsible for his safety."

It was March of Casey's first-grade year, and the principal was presiding over a meeting that included Casey's teacher, occupational therapist, guidance counselor, special education coordinator, parents, and psychologist. Casey was blowing up a lot less often at home, but there were still some kinks to work out at school.

"Well," the psychologist said, "as you know, in some

ways Casey's leaving the classroom is more adaptive than some of the other things he could be doing in response to frustration—like tearing the room apart. But, I agree, it's very important that he stay safe."

"What's making Casey act this way?" asked the classroom teacher. "What's his diagnosis?"

"Well, I don't think a diagnosis will tell us much about why he's acting that way. But I think it's safe to say he's having a lot of trouble shifting from one mind-set to another and that he's not very good at solving problems," the psychologist said.

"So why does he run out of the room?" asked the teacher.

"Because he can't think of anything else to do," the psychologist said.

"I think we need to start solving some of the problems that are causing Casey to get so frustrated that he can't think of anything to do but run out of the room," said the psychologist. "But he may not stop running out of the room completely yet, so we may need a place where he can go to settle down when he does feel overwhelmed, so he doesn't end up in the parking lot."

The special education coordinator chimed in. "I think we should have consequences if he leaves the classroom," she said. "I don't think it's good for the other kids to see him leave when he gets frustrated."

"Why, have any of the other kids expressed a desire or shown an inclination to leave the classroom when they're frustrated?" the psychologist asked.

"No," said the teacher.

"Do we think Casey is leaving the classroom because he'd rather be out in the hallway all by himself?" the psychologist asked.

"I don't think so," said the teacher. "He's always very eager to come back in as soon as he's settled down."

"Do we think that punishing him after he leaves the classroom will have any effect on his behavior the next time he's frustrated and feels the need to leave the classroom?" the psychologist asked.

"I don't know," said the teacher. "It's almost as if he's in a completely different zone when he's frustrated."

"Then I'm not certain why we'd punish Casey for leaving the classroom," the psychologist continued. "Especially if the main reason we're doing it is to set an example for the other kids."

"So what do you suggest we do when he gets frustrated?" asked the special education coordinator.

"I think most of our energy should be focused on what to do before Casey gets frustrated, not after," the psychologist said. "When Casey's frustration with a particular task or situation is predictable, we can solve the problem that's routinely frustrating him ahead of time so he won't get to the point where he needs to run out of the classroom. If we should happen to run into an unpredictable frustration, I think we need a place for Casey to go to calm down if your initial efforts to calm him down don't do the trick. I don't think he's at the point yet where he's able to talk things through when he's frustrated, although we're working on it. Luckily, he's pretty good at calming down on his own if we leave him alone for a while. We have to find ways to let him do that while still making sure he's safe. So for now, our top priority is to keep explosions to a minimum, even at the expense of his learning. It's the explosions that are getting in the way of Casey's learning anyway."

Things went quite well for Casey for the last few months of that school year. At the beginning of the next school year the group reassembled, including his old and new teachers, reviewed what worked and what didn't the previous school year, and agreed to try to do more of the same, while focusing on helping Casey complete more schoolwork. Although we expected some rough moments as Casey adjusted to his new teachers and classmates, it wasn't until two months into the school year that he had his first series of explosions. The special education coordinator hastily called a meeting.

"We think Casey has regressed," the principal said. "He looks as bad as he did last school year."

"Actually, we think he looks a lot better than he did

last school year," said Casey's father. "In fact, we were happy he started off as well as he did. He was really looking forward to going back to school."

"I think we need to revisit the idea of consequences," said the special education coordinator. "Do you folks say anything to him about this behavior at home?" she asked the parents.

"Of course we do!" said the mother, a little offended. "We let him know very clearly that it is unacceptable, and he gets very upset because he knows that already. Believe me, this is being addressed at home."

"Is he exploding a lot at home?" asked the principal.

"We haven't had a major explosion in months," said the father. "We'd almost forgotten how bad things used to be."

"I still think Casey needs to know that at school, life doesn't just go on like nothing happened after he has a explosion," said the principal.

"I agree," said the special education coordinator.

"What did you have in mind?" asked the father.

"I think after he blows up, he needs to sit in my office and talk it over," said the principal. "And until he does, he shouldn't be permitted to rejoin his classmates."

"I don't think he's ready for that yet," the father said.

"Well," said the special education director, "whether

he's ready or not, it's important that the other students see that we disapprove of Casey's behavior."

"His classmates don't already know you disapprove of his behavior?" the psychologist asked.

"We think we need to send a stronger message," the special education coordinator said. "We think he can control this behavior."

"I think we should use consequences only if we believe that they will help Casey control himself the next time he gets frustrated," the psychologist said. "Otherwise consequences are only likely to make him more frustrated."

"We have to do what we think is right in our school," said the principal, ending the discussion.

Casey had a minor explosion two weeks later. He was escorted to the principal's office. The principal tried hard to get Casey to talk about his frustration. Casey couldn't. The principal insisted, setting the stage for a massive one-hour explosion that included spitting, swearing, and destroying property in the principal's office. Another meeting was hastily called.

"I've never been treated that way by a student!" said the principal. "Casey's going to have to understand that we can't accept that kind of behavior."

"Casey already knows that behavior is unacceptable!" said the mother. "Sometimes he can talk about what's frustrating him right away—and that's a recent development—but most of the time he can't talk about it until much later, and then we have to give him some time to collect himself before we try to help him."

"I tried that," said the principal. "When he was in my office, I told him that I wasn't going to talk to him until he was good and ready."

"How did he respond to that?" the psychologist asked.

"That's when he spit on me," said the principal.

"I guess that tells you that something about what you said made him more frustrated, not less," the psychologist said.

"You don't think having him sit in my office will eventually help?" asked the principal. "I'm very uncomfortable having him blow up and then watch him go happily out to recess and rejoin the other kids without there being some kind of consequence. I'm struggling with this."

"I think sitting in your office would work great if Casey experienced it as a place where he could calm down, rather than as a place where he's asked to do something he can't do yet—namely, talk about things immediately—or where he feels he's being punished for something he already knows he shouldn't have done."

"So why doesn't he just tell me he knows his behavior is unacceptable?" asked the principal.

"I don't think Casey can figure out why he behaves

in a way he knows is unacceptable," interjected the father. "After this recent episode, he was very upset. That night he practically begged me to give him more medicine so he wouldn't act that way anymore."

The assembled adults were silent for a brief moment.

"But I can't give the other children in his class the idea that they can do what he does and get away with it," said the principal.

"I honestly don't think that the students who are flexible and handle frustration well are going to start exploding just because they see Casey getting away with it," said the psychologist. "And he's not getting away with it. If you're teaching Casey how to deal more adaptively with frustration and solving the problems that cause him to explode, his classmates see that you take his explosions seriously, that you expect him not to explode, and that you know what you're doing. They won't think you know what you're doing if you make things worse."

Did Casey run out of the classroom again during the school year? Yes—to a designated desk in the hallway he knew was his "chill-out" area. Did he begin returning to the classroom much more rapidly after he left? Absolutely. Did he hit his principal again? No. Did he hit his classmates a few times? Yes—just like many of the other boys in his class. Did he continue to have trouble shifting gears? Yes, sometimes. But his teacher demonstrated to Casey that she could help him when he became frustrated, and Casey thrived in her class. One day I asked the teacher, "Do you think Casey's difficulties affect his relations with his peers?" She replied, "Oh, I think he's well liked despite his difficulties. I think the other kids can tell when Casey's having a rough day, and they try to help him make it through."

12

Now Is the Time

We've come a long way in eleven chapters. We started by taking a close look at different interpretations of and explanations for explosive behavior in children, emphasizing the fact that these interpretations and explanations greatly influence the ways in which we respond to such behavior and attempt to change it. You were encouraged to think about an explanation that represents a departure from conventional wisdom; namely, that explosive children are not choosing to explode, nor have they learned that exploding is an effective means of forcing adults to give in to their wishes but rather are delayed in the process of developing the skills that are critical to being flexible and tolerating frustration.

You were also encouraged to try on for size a new philosophy: *children do well if they can*. This is an important philosophy, for it suggests that if your child could do well, he would do well. In other words, he's already motivated not to explode and already knows you don't want him to. So using conventional reward and punishment strategies—consequences—to give him the incentive to do well or teach him that he shouldn't explode doesn't make a great deal of sense. These strategies often only heighten the likelihood of explosions. And, perhaps most important, these strategies don't teach him the thinking skills he lacks.

You were introduced to pathways (skills that need to be taught) and triggers (problems that need to be solved). Next, we began thinking about how to teach those skills and solve those problems while simultaneously reducing the likelihood of explosions and at the same time trying to help your child meet your expectations. You were introduced to three options for pursuing problems or unmet expectations with your child. With Plan A you're imposing your will (thereby pursuing your expectations but heightening the likelihood of explosions and teaching no skills). With Plan C, you're dropping the expectation, at least for now (thereby reducing the likelihood of an explosion but pursuing no expectations and teaching no skills). And with Plan B you're doing the name of the approach described in this book—Collaborative Problem Solving—thereby pursuing your expectations, reducing the likelihood of explosions, and teaching your child skills so that eventually he can do well in the real world without your help.

You read that there are two forms of Plan B: Proactive B and Emergency B. Because explosions are actually highly predictable, you learned that you should be solving most problems by doing Proactive B. We also reviewed the manner by which Plan B can be applied to sibling interactions, examined family communication patterns that can interfere with successful implementation of Plan B, and briefly discussed medications that are sometimes useful in addressing some of the pathways. And we took a look at how Plan B can improve life in school classrooms (in an era where the news media reports on preschoolers being suspended from school and elementary school children being taken from school in handcuffs, surely the time has come for a new way of doing things).

If you've been trying to implement this model in your home or classroom, you've probably been working pretty hard. That's OK—you were working hard already—let's just make sure you have something to show for all that hard work. Just remember, it can take a while. You don't fix a reading disability in a week, and you don't fix this learning disability in a week either. But if things aren't going as well as you'd hoped, seek out someone who can help you. Someone who knows that children do well if they can.

• • •

Perhaps you're wondering what happened to Jennifer, star of the waffle episode, which is where we started eleven chapters ago. She's working as a nanny to a one-year-old child while she figures out what she wants to do next. Does she still get pretty frustrated sometimes? Yes. Does she still explode? No.

"I used to spend so much energy being upset. Then I realized it wasn't doing me any good," she said recently. "Now if I get upset about something, a lot of times I'll just stop for a second and ask myself if being upset is going to make things any better. I've learned I have a pretty obsessive personality. If I'm upset about something, I can spend a lot of time thinking about it, so I try to do things that will take my mind off what I'm upset about."

Jennifer's mother often reflects on the road she and her daughter have traveled together.

"I want people who have a child like Jennifer to know that there is light at the end of the tunnel. The road isn't always easy—even today—but things are far better than we ever thought possible. Jennifer often thanks us for not giving up on her.

"I did have to come to grips with the fact that I didn't get the child I hoped for. And I had to have different priorities for Jennifer. Some things that I thought mattered a lot really didn't matter at all . . . not in the scheme of things, not with this child. And I know this is going to sound crazy, but I had to start finding humor in my situation. It's easy to get so wrapped up in the moment. But it's the big picture that matters. I held my family together. My marriage survived. My other kids turned out OK. And Jennifer is a wonderful young woman."

If you've also been thinking, "Shouldn't all children be raised this way?" the answer is "But of course." You see, while the CPS model has its roots in the treatment of explosive kids, it's clear that it's not just explosive kids who need help identifying their concerns; taking another person's concerns into account; expressing frustration in an adaptive manner; generating and considering alternative solutions to problems; working toward mutually satisfactory solutions; resolving disputes and disagreements without conflict. *All* kids need help with these skills.

We have the technology: *five pathways, three Plans,* and *three steps for doing Plan B*. If not now, when? If not you, who?

Children do well if they can. If they can't . . . well, now you know what to do.

Additional Resources and Support

Problem Solving/Difficult Kids

Kurcinka, M. S. *Raising Your Spirited Child: A Guide for Parents Whose Child Is More Intense, Sensitive, Perceptive, Persistent, and Energetic*. New York: HarperCollins, 1992.

Shure, M. *Raising a Thinking Child*. New York: Pocket/Simon & Schuster, 1994.

Waugh, L. D. *Tired of Yelling: Teaching Our Children to Resolve Conflict*. Marietta, GA: Longstreet, 1999.

Nonverbal Learning Disability

Stewart, K. *Helping a Child with Nonverbal Learning Disorder or Asperger's Syndrome: A Parent's Guide.* Oakland, CA: New Harbinger, 2002.

Rourke, B. *Nonverbal Learning Disabilities: The Syndrome and the Model.* New York: Guilford Press, 1989.

Social Skills

Carlsson-Paige, N., and D. E. Levin. *Before Push Comes to Shove: Building Conflict Resolution Skills with Children.* St. Paul, MN: Redleaf, 1998.

Nowicki, S., and M. Duke. *Helping the Child Who Doesn't Fit In.* Atlanta, GA: Peachtree Publishers, 1992.

Sensory Integration Dysfunction

Kranowitz, C. S. *The Out-of-Sync Child: Recognizing and Coping with Sensory Integration Dysfunction.* New York: Perigee Publishing, 1998.

Sibling Issues

Faber, A., and E. Mazlish. *Siblings Without Rivalry: How to Help Your Children Live Together So You Can Live Too*. New York: Avon Books, 1998.

Classroom and School Process

Kohn, A. *Beyond Discipline: From Compliance to Community*. Alexandria, VA: Association for Supervision and Curriculum Development, 1996.

Levin, D. E. *Teaching Young Children in Violent Times: Building a Peaceable Classroom*. Cambridge, MA: Educators for Social Responsibility, 1994.

Levin, J., and J. M. Shanken-Kaye. *The Self-Control Classroom: Understanding and Managing the Disruptive Behavior of All Students, Including Those with ADHD*. Dubuque, IA: Kendall/Hunt Publishing, 1996.

Noddings, N. *The Challenge to Care in Schools*. New York: Teachers College Press, 1992.

Wagner, T. *Making the Grade: Reinventing America's Schools*. New York: Routledge, 2001.

Psychopharmacology

Koplewicz, H. *It's Nobody's Fault: New Hope and Help for Difficult Children and Their Parents*. New York: Three Rivers Press, 1996.

Support

- Center for Collaborative Problem Solving www.ccps.info
- Collaborative Problem Solving Institute www.massgeneral.org/cpsinstitute
- Foundation for Children with Behavioral Challenges (FCBC) www.fcbcsupport.org
- Parents & Teachers of Explosive Kids (PTEK) www.explosivekids.org
- Tourette Syndrome Foundation of Canada www.tourette.ca
- Tourette Syndrome Association (TSA) www.tsa-usa.org
- Tourette Syndrome "Plus" www.tourettesyndrome.net

- Life's a Twitch www.lifesatwitch.com
- Nonverbal Learning Disability Association (NLDA) www.nlda.org
- Asperger Syndrome Coalition of the United States (ASC-U.S.) www.asperger.org
- Online Asperger Syndrome Information and Support (OASIS) www.udel.edu/bkirby/asperger
- MAAP Services for the Autism and Asperger Syndrome (The Source) www.maapservices.org
- Sensory Integration Network www.sinetwork.org
- Childhood Anxiety Network www.childhoodanxietynetwork.org
- Obsessive Compulsive Foundation www.ocfoundation.org
- Child and Adolescent Bipolar Foundation (CABF) www.cabf.org
- Children and Adults with Attention Deficit Disorder (CHADD) www.chadd.org

Index